Narrative Poems by
ALEXANDER
PUSHKIN
and by
MIKHAIL
LERMONTOV

Narrative Poems by
ALEXANDER PUSHKIN
and by
MIKHAIL LERMONTOV

Translated by

CHARLES JOHNSTON

Introduction by Kyril FitzLyon

Vintage Books
A Division of Random House
New York

FIRST VINTAGE BOOKS EDITION, November 1983

Library of Congress Cataloging in Publication Data
Main entry under title:

Narrative poems.

   Contents: Onegin's journey; Graf Nulin; Mozart and
Salieri; The bronze horseman / by Alexander Pushkin—
The Tambov lady; The novice; The demon / by
Mikhail Lermontov.
   1. Russian poetry—19th century—Translations into
English.   2. English poetry—Translations from
Russian.   I. Pushkin, Aleksandr Sergeevich, 1799–1837.
Poems. English. Selections. 1983. II. Lermontov,
Mikhail IŪr'evich, 1814–1841. Poems. English. Selections.
1983. III. Johnston, Charles Hepburn, Sir, 1912–
[PG3347.A17   1983b]   891.71'3'08   83-48065
ISBN 0-394-72097-0 (pbk.)

Manufactured in the United States of America

CONTENTS

INTRODUCTION

Onegin's Journey, which opens this collection of Sir Charles Johnston's translations of Russian poetry, has had a curious history. Pushkin originally intended it to follow Chapter Seven of *Eugene Onegin*, in which Tatyana is taken to Moscow and meets "that fat general," Prince N., whom she eventually marries. The present Chapter Eight would then have become Chapter Nine. However, for reasons which he said were "important to him, but not to the public," Pushkin decided to omit *Onegin's Journey*. But when a friendly critic pointed out that this made "the transition from Tatyana, the provincial young girl, to Tatyana, the grand lady," too abrupt and unexplained, Pushkin compromised by publishing some of the *Journey* stanzas as a kind of appendix to Chapter Eight. These are the stanzas that Charles Johnston translated and published some two years after his translation of *Eugene Onegin*,* and which appear in the present collection. (Additional stanzas were published after Pushkin's death.)

It is not possible to guess with any degree of confidence at the reasons that prompted Pushkin to discard *Onegin's Journey*, and which he found so "important." He may have thought it broke the poem's mold either stylistically or by straying too far from the subject, or both these things at once. For its subject matter and perhaps for inspiration, he had drawn on his memories of visits he himself had made to the Crimea and the Caucasus, and he was able to include some stanzas he had written five years previously describing his own stay in Odessa.

Eugene Onegin's final chapter (now renumbered Chapter

---

* *Eugene Onegin* by Alexander Pushkin, translated by Charles Johnston (London, 1977; New York, 1978; Penguin Classics, 1979).

Eight) and "fragments"—Pushkin's expression—of *Onegin's Journey* were published in 1832. The year 1827 (five years before) saw the publication of *Graf Nulin,* which introduces a new genre into Russian poetry—the anecdotal. It was a genre Pushkin was to repeat (on a different theme and in a different metre) in *The Little House in Kolomna* and which was to find imitators in Lermontov and Turgenev.

Graf Nulin is based on Shakespeare's *The Rape of Lucrece.* As much, that is, as a joke can be based on a tragedy. In December 1825, says Pushkin in a note discovered among his papers, he was rereading Shakespeare's poem (which he found "pretty feeble," partly, no doubt, because he was reading it in a French translation) when it occurred to him that world history would have been different if only Lucrece had slapped Tarquin's face as he was about to rape her. It would probably have cooled his ardour, she would not have committed suicide, and Rome would not have become a republic. "The idea came to me," says Pushkin, "of parodying history and Shakespeare. I couldn't resist the double temptation and wrote this story in a couple of mornings." Later he admitted to a further English literary influence. Byron's *Beppo,* he wrote, was another source of his inspiration for *Graf Nulin.* For his "parody" he chose not world history, kings, captains, and beautiful high-born ladies, all in classical antiquity, but the modest contemporary background of a Russian country house, a bored young woman whose husband is absent not on affairs of state or war, but merely on a hunting expedition, and a fashionable fop (his name means "zero") delighted at the prospect of an easy lay.

A number of small details in *Lucrece* and *Graf Nulin* resemble one another, but often the resemblances are seen as in a distorting mirror. Tarquin, on his way from his own bed to Lucrece's, throws "his mantle rudely o'er his arm" and creeps stealthily from room to room, nervously mindful of "grating" doors. Nulin, in a similar situation, grabs his "bright silk dressing gown" and is "in mortal terror" of creaking floor-boards as he sets out on his escapade. Both these unworthy heroes are compared to a tomcat, yet Tarquin, unlike poor Nulin, is also a "grim lion [who] fawneth o'er his prey." Both wives inform their husbands after the event, though not quite in the same spirit, but then the events differ too. Tarquin achieves his goal—with momentous consequences for himself, Lucrece, and the world; Nulin achieves nothing except a slap in the face.

Pushkin's poem had a mixed reception on publication. The more serious critics found it immoral as well as too flippant for a great national poet (aged twenty-six). But a few reviewers praised it, and the public loved it. So, fortunately for Pushkin, did the emperor Nicholas I. He had constituted himself Push-kin's personal censor and had seen the poem in manuscript, thought it "delightful," and asked Benckendorff, his formida-ble chief of police, to inform Pushkin that he had read it "with great pleasure." His verdict has been echoed by every reader of Pushkin ever since.

Five years later it was Barry Cornwall's turn to attract Pushkin's attention. Pushkin continued to admire him quite literally to his dying day. His last letter, written a few hours before his fatal duel, was addressed to Alexandra Ishin, a well-known translator, urging her to translate Barry Cornwall's *Dramatic Scenes* and apologising for not bringing her the vol-ume himself for lack of time.

Pushkin's now almost forgotten English contemporary—somewhat older than he, though he died many years later—Bryan Procter (Barry Cornwall's real name) achieved in his day (1787–1874) considerable popularity both at home and abroad. His *Dramatic Scenes* suggested to Pushkin his own *Little Tragedies,* short pieces which are, in fact, character stud-ies designed to show the effect of some particular passion on human behaviour. One of them, *Mozart and Salieri,* a study of envy, is based on the entirely groundless, but at that time fairly widely believed, rumour that Salieri had murdered Mozart by poisoning him. (In Beethoven's Conversation Book for 1823, only seven years before Pushkin composed his poem, the rumour is attributed to Salieri himself.) Pushkin's Salieri is a sensitive and intelligent man of considerable talent and fine musical discrimination: he acknowledges his rival's greatness and realizes his superiority to himself. But his appreciation of art, though subtle and acute, is exercised at the cost of all his other faculties. Mozart, on the other hand, less intelligent, perhaps, than Salieri, has something more than intelligence or even talent. He has genius. This gives him a freedom of attitude to life and the world around him: art is for him vitally important, but at the same time, it forms a part of life as a whole. He feels no need to scoff at a blind street violinist, as does Salieri, just because the violinist makes a hash of one of Mozart's own melodies; in fact, he enjoys it. He can always find time to play with his little son, or warn his wife about supper, instead of neglecting these things in the interest of musical composition. This, Pushkin implies, is the fundamental antithesis dividing talent from genius. Talent can be both inventive and productive, yet, for all its inventiveness, it is constricting because it obeys other men's rules. Genius is free and, therefore, liberating, because it is spontaneous and unlaboured, welling up from a man's innermost being, accepting the world in its totality and creating works of art which are genuine because they obey rules laid down by their creator and not by someone else.

It is interesting to note that Salieri's criticism of Mozart—he is too flippant, too careless of his own gifts, unworthy of himself—is very similar to the criticism levelled at Pushkin by some of his contemporaries. Pushkin obviously felt Mozart to be a kindred spirit, and this particular "Little Tragedy" may justifiably be interpreted as his answer to his critics.

Mozart and Salieri was written in 1830. Three years later

Pushkin wrote what was to be his last (and shortest) narrative poem, *The Bronze Horseman*, considered by many to be his finest poetic achievement. Though it was written in 1833, its publication was held up by censorship for eight years, and when it did finally appear—posthumously—it was somewhat disfigured by changes introduced to placate the censor. In a completely unbowdlerised form it was published for the first time only in 1904. Its language is, for the most part, sober and direct, sometimes colloquial (as so much of Russian poetry is, not only Pushkin's), and the situations and the description of them are entirely realistic. In fact, to describe some of them Pushkin drew upon reports and specialist literature of the time, making use of the vocabulary and the expressions he found there.

The story is simple enough. In the great flood that overwhelmed St. Petersburg (Pushkin, by the way, was the first to call it Petrograd) in 1824 when the river Nevá burst its banks, Evgeny, a poor, insignificant clerk, loses his girl and his reason. He curses Peter the Great, the city's founder, for being the prime cause of his misfortunes, and shakes his fist at Peter's monument—the Bronze Horseman—whereupon he fancies that the statue comes to life and gallops after him through the streets. Eventually he dies without recovering his sanity.

The long and magnificent Introduction to the poem, describing Peter's thoughts as he surveys the bleak and deserted Baltic shore where he plans to build his new capital, the role played in the poem by the river and the city, which are presented almost like living creatures with a will of their own (in Johnston's translation the river "pounces" on the city, "mad as a beast," the waves are "malicious" and "like thieves, burst in through windows," St. Petersburg—"Triton-Petropol"—surfaces "with waters lapping round his waist")—all this gives the poem several *dramatis personae* on a par with Evgeny, all interacting with each other: Evgeny himself, the Nevá, the city, Peter as ruler and as the Bronze Horseman come to life in Ev-

geny's imagination. At the same time, in the course of compos-
ing the poem, as one version succeeded another, Pushkin gradu-
ally stripped Evgeny of his individuality to the point of
depriving him of all distinctive features and even of his sur-
name, which he was allowed to have in the earlier versions, but
which in the final version "is not required." Evgeny starts off
by being a rich young man, but in each successive version he
becomes poorer, goes down in the social scale, and gradually
loses all personal characteristics. Descriptions of his physical
appearance and even of his room become ever sparser, until at
last they disappear altogether and he becomes almost an ab-
straction, certainly no less so than the Bronze Horseman. The
two protagonists—the mighty emperor and the insignificant
clerk—are now seen on the same plane, like two contrasting but
equal principles.

In fact, it was as a conflict of two principles that the poem
was almost immediately perceived by Russian critics: the State
or the collective principle on the one hand, the heroic principle,
the individual, on the other. What the critics could not agree on
was the assignment of roles. Belinsky, writing soon after the
publication of the poem in 1841, had no doubts at all on that
score. The representative of the collective will was obviously
Peter. He embodied the State, revolutionised the lives of its cit-
izens by his reforms, and built his city, the symbol of it all, in
obedience to historical necessity, despite the cries and protests
of the individual, the miserable and helpless clerk of the poem,
crushed by the impersonal forces of the *raison d'état,* beyond
his control and understanding. The wretched victim is, in his
way, a hero, as he throws out his challenge to the Bronze Horse-
man, "the Idol," even though he flees in terror when he fancies
he sees the Idol's head turn towards him in anger.

Later critics reverse the roles. To them the heroic principle is
personified by Peter. His is the triumph of the individual will
over the collective, over that impersonal and helpless mass so

well represented by the pathetic figure of Evgeny, whose happiness and, in the end, life itself are destroyed by the consequences of Peter's policy, symbolised by St. Petersburg.

At the turn of the present century this interpretation was further developed and given a fashionably revolutionary twist. Evgeny, the representative, according to this theory, of the democratic masses, is, these critics stress, not only treated by Pushkin on the same level as Peter, the embodiment of autocracy, but even made to threaten the Tsar with vague future vengeance for all his (i.e., the autocracy's) misdemeanours. "Take care!" he hisses, "you'll get your deserts yet!" (Charles Johnston translates the last half-dozen words—only two in Russian—by the equally menacing and indeterminate single word: "when ...") And the Tsar, the Idol astride his bronze horse, so calm and aloof, *au-dessus de la mêlée,* at the beginning of the poem when his back is turned to Evgeny in contemptuous indifference, can no longer feel safe and unconcerned "atop his rock, fenced-off." He leaps over the protective railings and pursues the rebel in order to crush him. He succeeds, in a sense: Evgeny *is* crushed—he dies demented and unmourned, society's reject. But his threat, the threat of the victimised masses thirsting to square their accounts with the autocracy, remains as real as ever. The message is clear: the autocracy will not forever remain on its rocklike, seemingly impregnable pedestal, protected by railings of power, high above the masses, aloof and indifferent to them. Henceforth it will have to fight for its position—or even existence—or disappear.

Is this really what Pushkin had in mind? And if he had, did he think the autocracy might lose the next round? There is no means of knowing. But those who are inclined to think he had and did, could point to a drawing by him, found among his papers, representing Peter's monument in St. Petersburg: the great rock, which serves as a pedestal, and the horse. But there is no one sitting on it. The bronze horse has lost its rider.

Pushkin's *Bronze Horseman* had not yet been cleared by the censor when Lermontov (1814–41) finished his final version of *Mtsyri,* Georgian for "novice," the title under which Charles Johnston presents his translation. It was Lermontov's third attempt at the same theme: the confession of a man in search of inner freedom. The first attempt was entitled *The Confession.* He wrote it at the precociously early age of fifteen to sixteen, but never completed it. He did the second version (*The Boyar Orsha*) five years later, but was not, it seems, entirely satisfied with it. In 1837, just four years before his death in a duel at the age of twenty-six, Lermontov visited an ancient monastery in Georgia, deserted by all but one monk. The monk told him the story of his life, and it was under the impression of that story, which he left essentially unaltered since it coincided with his own concept of himself, that Lermontov wrote *The Novice.*

Its composition was thus more or less contemporaneous with Pushkin's *Bronze Horseman,* but the gulf that separates the two is unbridgeably wide. Pushkin's vision, tinged, as it is, with Romanticism, is still predominantly classical. Clarity, terseness, objectivity are its hallmarks. Lermontov's is entirely Romantic and, therefore, entirely subjective. Stylistically, he is interested not in precision or *le mot juste* but in the total impression. His poetry seems to gush out in intermittent torrents in which the sense often depends on general effect, not to be too closely scrutinised for faults of detail or logic or even consistency. Nowhere is this more evident than in *The Demon.*

Absorbed as Lermontov is by his own emotions, attitudes, desires, unhappiness, his theme is basically almost always himself. (*"Moi,"* he once confessed in a private letter, *"c'est la personne que je fréquente avec le plus de plaisir."*) *The Novice* is no exception. It mirrors the Romantic's and Lermontov's own protest against his pattern of life and his lot in it, his revolt against accepted values, his craving for freedom, and his resentment based on the disillusionment, so typical of Lermon-

tov's generation (both in Russia and elsewhere), which fol-
lowed that of the French Revolution, when hopes rode high of a
new heaven and a new earth. It is not difficult to interpret *The
Novice* as Lermontov's spiritual and psychological autobiogra-
phy, with his deeply ingrained pessimism, his rootlessness, his
sense of isolation and loneliness, so much in tune with the Ro-
mantic mood of the time. The novice of the poem, too, is imbued
with a feeling of "otherness" which keeps him aloof from the
monks who have brought him up and among whom he lives. He
makes his bid for freedom, but it is an ineffectual bid, and it
lands him back at his starting point because he loses his way, a
symbol of the futility of life with no more meaning to it than
that of a squirrel running around its wheel in a cage. Only in
death can the novice hope to find his release.

Of course, like all great poems, this one, too, allows various
interpretations. It is, for instance, not unusual, though I dis-
agree with it, to give it a political connotation. The novice's
monastery is seen not as the world in which man is held cap-
tive, misunderstood by his fellow-men, alienated and ulti-
mately alone till death rescues him from it—a typically
Romantic attitude—but in more robust terms, as the Russian
Empire's grip on the Caucasus after the cession of Georgia to
the Tsar in 1801.

Georgia and the Caucasus had for Lermontov, as indeed for
most Russians and particularly the Romantics, an irresistible
appeal. It is not surprising, therefore, that *The Demon*, Ler-
montov's greatest poem (and to many Russians, whether justi-
fiably or not, the greatest poem in the Russian language),
should have the Caucasus as its background. It occupied Ler-
montov all his short adult life from the age of fifteen to within a
few months of his death a dozen years later, passing through
eight different versions with major alterations in five of them.
There is, of course, no certainty that even the final version
would have stayed unaltered if the poet's life had been spared.

Besides, as the poem was not published in Lermontov's life-time, the manuscript copies that circulated in Russia were in-evitably faulty and contained a number of alternative readings which continue to plague editors to this day.

The poem had a vast and immediate success. Belinsky, the fa-mous mid-nineteenth-century Russian literary critic who was apt to judge literature in social or political terms, interpreted it as a passionate call to freedom, while his generally hostile at-titude to religion made him prefer those versions of it which could be interpreted as expressing religious doubts on the part of the author. In accordance with this preference, the Soviet Academy edition has restored some of the lines omitted by Ler-montov, presumably out of censorship considerations, from his last draft, lines in which Lucifer ("the Demon") assures Ta-mara that God cares "for heaven, but not for earth." In Charles Johnston's translation they are enclosed in square brackets.

Like Pushkin's *Eugene Onegin, The Demon* is a novel in prose, but unlike *Eugene Onegin,* it represents the very quin-tessence of Romanticism. It is the story of Lucifer's passionate love for a beautiful Georgian princess whom he is able to se-duce, after she has fled from him to a convent and taken her mo-nastic vows, by promises of unearthly delights and of his own regeneration as a result of which evil would vanish from this world. After her death, however, he is balked of his prize, for her soul is carried off by an angel of God. The story is based on an ancient Georgian legend according to which love for a mor-tal woman, if reciprocated, can save Lucifer from himself and restore him to his former place in the divine hierarchy as one of God's archangels, so that evil would disappear from among men.

But Lermontov's Lucifer or Demon, unlike Milton's, is not an entirely divine—even if negatively divine—supernatural figure. He is a man writ large—very large indeed—and there-fore not entirely cut off from mankind, but linked to it, as Milton's Lucifer is not, by his emotions, his hopes, his readiness to abjure his power. The country he visits is a real country, so much so, in fact, that in the view of one literary critic, the poem's description of it could be used as a topographical guide to the Caucasus. Besides, the language, though often sublime, is at the same time natural. All this establishes a rapport between the Demon and the reader, a possibility for the reader to recognize his own sentiments, emotions, and desires and, therefore, to participate in the Demon's, though aware, of course, of his own obvious inferiority. But however grand the passion or, for that matter, the disillusionment of the Demon, Lermontov never completely loses touch with his tendency towards realism.

This tendency is given full vent in *The Tambov Lady*. In Lermontov's *oeuvre* it preceded *The Novice* (though not *The Demon*) and was probably written over a period of two years: January 1836 to January 1838, when Lermontov was a very young man of between twenty-one and twenty-three. His reputation was growing rapidly, and after Pushkin's death (like his own—in a duel) in January 1837, he was increasingly looked upon as the older poet's literary successor. The radical magazine *Sovremennik* (*The Contemporary*) published the poem almost immediately after it was finished, but, unfortunately, it was badly mauled by government censorship and by editorial cuts, reaching its readers in a mutilated state, to Lermontov's understandable fury. Since the author's manuscript has not survived, it has never been possible to repair the damage satisfactorily. One editor of Lermontov's complete works (P. Viskovatov, Moscow, 1891) tried to do so by restoring to the text passages which a cousin of Lermontov's happened to remember by heart—or said he did. Other editors have suggested that Viskovatov himself may have contributed to the restoration. In any case, there can be no guarantee of authenticity. Besides, the cousin's memory (and, perhaps, Viskovatov's inspiration) did not stretch to all the lines excised by the editor and the censor, and the gaps in the poem, as it has come down to us, are annoyingly numerous.

Though *The Tambov Lady* is not written in direct imitation of Pushkin, it follows the metric scheme of *Eugene Onegin,* and, in its description of the birthday ball and the guests at the Treasurer's house, presumably quite deliberately echoes the passages in *Eugene Onegin* dealing with the festivities in the Larins' country house on the occasion of Tatyana's name-day. But Lermontov's satire is more biting. Not one of *The Tambov Lady* characters, whether major or minor, escapes with any degree of credit, though the Lady herself has her moment of dignity at the very end.

The dramatic climax of the story—husband losing wife at cards—may have been suggested to Lermontov by Hoffmann's story "Spielerglück" (Hoffmann was immensely popular in Russia at the time), in which a man similarly gambles away his wife. The situation strikes the modern reader as ludicrously impossible, a Gogol-like absurdity. It was, of course, grotesque even at the time it was written, but it was so in the sense in which a caricature is (or is meant to be) grotesque. In other words, it had a reference, however distorted or obscure, to real life or, more exactly, to certain facets of it. The reference (which nowadays might have been to bingo or to football pools) was to the then universal, in some cases all-absorbing passion for card games which, since the preceding century, when in Russia imitation of all things Western became the order of the day, had held Russian urban society in its grip. Ordinary mortals could not, like Louis XIV on a famous occasion, pledge their country's budget at the gaming table, but the more dishonest did the next best thing by trying to recoup their losses at the expense of such public funds as they had access to. The Tambov Lady's husband could not compete with Louis XIV, but as District Treasurer he did enjoy obvious opportunities which he did not neglect. For he, after all,

long years with the official treasure
had lived as if it were his own.

Others, not so lucratively placed, could and did stake and lose
their entire personal fortunes or were driven to commit or at
least contemplate crime, like Herman in Pushkin's *Queen of
Spades* (familiar to opera lovers), another Russian nineteenth-
century literary masterpiece where a game of cards plays the
central role.

The language of *The Tambov Lady* is not merely collo-
quial—the language of Russian poetry often is—but conversa-
tional and even, on occasion, slangy. Besides, the Lady herself
does not conform to the usual Romantic pattern. She may be
pretty and attractive, but she does not sit by the window in
perfect idleness dreaming dreams of love or reading *La nou-
velle Héloïse* by Jean Jacques Rousseau. She sits there knitting
a stocking or maybe darning it, obviously careful not to waste
her time. This realism, both linguistic and descriptive, the
finely observed details, the ability to convey the atmosphere of
provincial society, not only render the caricature convincing,
but make the poem into a landmark in Lermontov's develop-
ment from poet to novelist—and author of *A Hero of Our Time.*
But whatever the potentialities of Lermontov's literary talent
might have been, they had hardly time to develop, let alone be
realised to anything like their full measure, in the course of the
very few years he had at his disposal.

1983   Kyril FitzLyon

TRANSLATOR'S NOTE

Besides dealing with texts and with the technical problems of translation, this note also contains some comments on the substance of the poems translated—to be read as a personal supplement to Kyril FitzLyon's illuminating introduction.

That short but delicious Pushkinian reject, *Onegin's Journey*, is a travel story, and lacks the drama and tension of *Eugene Onegin* itself. Otherwise, however, it has all the characteristics of Pushkin's poetic novel—the freshness, the mordant wit, the lyrical response to scenery, both rural and urban, the Byronic raciness, the tearaway sense of enjoyment. In particular, the account of Pushkin's day in Odessa (**XXIV–XXIX**) forms a high-spirited counterpart to the rollicking story of Onegin's Petersburg routine in Chapter One of the main poem.

In translating *Onegin's Journey* I have made full use of the unrhymed translation and the invaluable notes as well as the Russian text in Volumes 1, 3, and 4 of Vladimir Nabokov's edition of *Eugene Onegin* (London: Routledge and Kegan Paul, 1964; revised edition, 1976).

As for *Graf Nulin*, Pushkin's debonair fable about a virtuous wife, with its hilariously deadpan conclusion, in seeking to convey the racy tone of the original I have deliberately used an idiom which includes reminiscences of P. G. Wodehouse ("the housewife's optic") and of the bar-room talk in James Joyce's *Dubliners* ("strengthened by a tincture"). If in so doing I should upset some of Pushkin's devotees, I suspect that the Master himself might have looked on this proceeding with a tolerant eye. I make no apology for using three Russian words in all their indigenous vigour: *tsap*, with its combined suggestion of snatching and scratching, far more appropriate than the rough English equivalent *snap* when it comes to a cat catching a mouse; *durák,* so much more expressive than *fool;* and *ko-lyaska,* the sound of which implies a rolling, rattling progress more vividly than *carriage* (to say nothing about the difficulty of finding a suitable English rhyme for *Vaska*).

The theme of *Mozart and Salieri,* that subtle study of the confrontation between talent and genius, is already familiar to playgoers from Peter Shaffer's *Amadeus.* In John Bayley's words, Pushkin's version embodies "a legend dramatised with elegant intensity."

The Bronze Horseman is particularly hard to translate, and I offer my version of it with the greatest diffidence. It is a noble work, though lacking in that light relief which, say in *Eugene Onegin* or *Graf Nulin,* is so refreshing to the translator. It exemplifies brilliantly a combination of qualities in Pushkin which, I say in all humility, makes me feel particularly close to him: a robust, almost jingoistic patriotism—and a keen sense for the arrogant ugliness of absolute power.

In translating all three of these poems I have used the edition of Pushkin's collected works published by A. S. Suvorin in St. Petersburg in 1887.

Now for Lermontov. I have called the first poem of his in this selection *The Tambov Lady* because his exact title, *The Treasurer's Wife of Tambov,* seemed to me cumbersome and forbidding when rendered literally into English. It is a rattling yarn, told in the fast-moving *Eugene Onegin* metre, with, as Kyril FitzLyon says, a strongly novelistic element that gives us, as it were, a preview of Lermontov the author of *A Hero of Our Time.* As a man who had moved in high circles in St. Petersburg, Lermontov describes the boredom and pretentious second-rateness of Tambov society with a sort of fascinated horror. The Guard Hussars, with their scarlet dolmans, had been his own regiment—until he was transferred to a less elegant unit in the Caucasus because the poem he wrote following Pushkin's death was regarded by the authorities as subversive. In his digression about the cavalry trumpets which herald the Marshal's dinner party in Tambov (stanza **XXIX**), Lermontov expresses the full force of the nostalgia he felt for a sort of social and regimental Paradise Lost. The poem is, of course, deeply influenced by *Eugene Onegin*—but it was written about ten years later and contains a new ingredient which is alien to Pushkin's Mozartian limpidity: a strain of almost Gothic romance. (For example, the stilted quality of Garin's speech to his loved one in stanza **XXXVI** would have been unthinkable in the mouth of Onegin.) In fact the extraordinary flavour of *The Tambov Lady* derives largely from the manner in which such romanticism is combined with the chillingly realistic account of the siege laid by Garin to the heroine. This part of the poem—with Lermontov's commentary on the proceedings—reads like a manual for seducers. Given the conventions of the day, of course, such a siege—if successful—could hardly have ended otherwise than as it did, in the Hoffmannesque fantasy of the Treasurer losing his wife to Garin at cards, in the lady's melodramatic swoon, and in the teasing reticence of the final stanza. What happened, indeed? For a possible answer we can turn to Tolstoy, whose *Anna Karenina* so curiously parallels Lermontov's story and develops its potential.

Lermontov's Petersburg snobbery made him despise Tambov, but it did nothing to diminish his enthusiasm for the Caucasus. That chain of glittering, snowy peaks dominates his finest writing in both verse and prose. His Muse awaited him there—and so did his fate.

Although as a regimental officer Lermontov took part bravely in imperial Russia's conquest of the Caucasus, *The Novice* shows him as warmly sympathetic to the fate of the vanquished. The stifling cloister in which the boy-captive is confined sets the tone of the poem as a whole and even influences its metrical structure: the feminine rhyme (*pleasure/measure*) is absent and, as Turgenev says in the foreword to his French translation,* "This form, by its very monotony, lends the poem a special energy. It has been compared to the sound of a prisoner hammering incessantly on the walls of his cell."

The Demon inevitably invites comparison with *Eugene Onegin*. The Demon himself has been called a sort of airborne Onegin; he has not only Eugene's pride and wickedness but also his keen sense of enjoyment and his capacity for affection. For her part, in each poem, the heroine develops almost out of recognition: Pushkin's Tatyana, from shy provincial miss to social ruler of St. Petersburg and "law-giver of the Nevá"; Lermontov's Tamara, from the infantile fascinator dancing at the wedding party to the mature and passionate woman who is capable of answering the Demon in his own sophisticated language and of influencing him—momentarily—for good.

There is, however, a major difference in tone between the two poems. *Onegin* is conversationally expressed, and often extremely funny: mocking, cynical, witty to the point of buffoonery. It laughs at everything, including itself. *The Demon*, by contrast, is on a high level of seriousness: the note of *gravitas* is sustained throughout. This increases the danger to which the verse translator is congenitally exposed: the hazard of bathos. More specifically, it is the feminine rhyme which, as in *Onegin*, gives the translator the most trouble. The perennial problem of preventing a takeover by the jolly Victorian jingle is compounded in this case by the elevated tone of the poem. The higher the wire, the harder the fall.

> "I would not be remotely human
> did I not love the little woman"

is bad enough when sung by General Prince Gremin in the last act of Tchaikovsky's operatic version of *Onegin*. A corresponding protestation in the mouth of Lermontov's Demon would just about put the hosts of heaven and hell out of business.

Some translators, notably Messrs. L'Ami and Welikotny, *Michael Lermontov, Biography and Translation* (Winnipeg: University of Manitoba Press, 1967), have solved the difficulty by cutting out the feminine rhyme almost entirely. As I have indicated above, Lermontov himself did this, with deliberate purpose, in *The Novice;* but for *The Demon* I have thought it best to follow Lermontov's rhyming scheme as closely as possible; without the feminine rhyme the poem would acquire a monotony which, in this case, Lermontov did not intend, and would lose much of its demoniac vitality.

The version of *The Demon* used in the present translation is that published by the Academy of Sciences of the U.S.S.R. in 1955* (*Lermontov, Poems,* Volume 4); it follows that edition in omitting from the text the different dedications which appear in the various drafts, and in including the lines "Why should I share your griefs . . . if we both are there?" (section X), but in square brackets, to indicate that Lermontov cut them out of his last draft. For *The Novice* and *The Tambov Lady* I have used the text in Volume 2 of the 1962 edition of the U.S.S.R. Academy of Sciences.

1983   C.H.J.

---

* I have preferred a different reading at one point only. In IV 6, the 1955 edition has *rainy,* poplars; I have substituted *ruiny,* ruins, the version in the second edition of Lermontov's poems, published by Wolfgang Gerhard, Leipzig, 1879.

Narrative Poems by
ALEXANDER
PUSHKIN
and by
MIKHAIL
LERMONTOV

ONEGIN'S JOURNEY

I–VIII

E. Onegin drives from Moscow
to Nizhny Novgorod.

IX

– – – – – – – – – – – – – – – – – – –
– – – – – – – – – – – – – before his eyes
Makaryev market hums and buzzes,
and seethes, and bursts with merchandise.
The Indian's brought here pearls like carrots,
the European—dubious clarets;
the steppeland breeder's come to town
with strings of horses (broken down),
and here are cards, the gamester's passion,
with handfuls of conniving dice;
the steppe landowner's brought his nice
ripe daughters, dressed in last year's fashion.
All's trade, and lies enough for two,
and noise, and general how d'you do.

X–XI

Boredom! . . .
Onegin travels to Astrakhan, and from there to
the Caucasus.

XII

He sees proud Terek,* magisterial,
gnaw the steep confines of its bed;
up here, an eagle planes, imperial,
a stag stands there with lowered head.
In cliff-shadow, a camel's lying;
through fields a Cherkess horse is flying;
round tents of a nomadic breed
the sheepflocks of the Kalmuck feed.
Far off loom the Caucasian masses;
their road is open. War has pried
its way through their age-old divide,
across their barriers and crevasses.
Arágva[†] and Kurá have now
seen Russian tents upon their brow.

XIII

But soon, above his desert sector,
while foothills all around him press,
Beshtú,[‡] serrated old protector,
stands with Mashúk of the green dress,
Mashúk, the source of healing rivers;
about his streams, those charmed life-givers,
swarm the pale orders of the faint,
victims of battle's proud complaint,
of kidneys, or of Aphrodite;

---

* Terek: A river rising on the north side of the Caucasus and flowing through Vladikavkaz into the Caspian Sea.
† Arágva and Kurá: Rivers rising south of the Caucasus and flowing through Georgia into the Caspian.
‡ Beshtú and Mashúk: Peaks overlooking Pyatigorsk, a mineral-spring in the northern Caucasus.

some think their life is like a length
of thread, the waves will give it strength;
coquettes hope the débris of flighty
decades will wash right off; old men
want, for a trice, youth back again.

XIV

Inspired to embittered meditation,
amidst this pitiable brigade,
Onegin with commiseration
questions the smoking stream, dismayed
by mists of gloom that hold him under:
Why have I no chest-wound, I wonder?
Why, like that tax-farmer, can't I
be old and doddering? Or why
on earth can't I be paralytic,
like Tula's councillor, or if not
why couldn't I at least have got
a shoulder that's a touch arthritic?
Oh God, I'm young, I'm fresh, I'm strong—
and I've got boredom, all day long.

Onegin then visits Tauris*

XV

_ _ _ _ _ _ _ _ _ _ _ _ _ _ _ _
_ _ _ _ _ _ _ _ _ _ _ _ _ _ _ _
_ _ _ _ _ _ _ _ _ _ _ _ _ _ _ _
_ _ _ _ _ _ _ _ _ _ _ _ _ _ _ _
scene, sacred to the imagination,

* Tauris: The Crimea.

of Mithridates'* suicide;
here Pylad† and Orestes vied,
and Mickiéwicz,‡ at the inspiration
of cliffs that beetle more and more,
recalled his Lithuanian shore.

XVI

Coasts of Tauris, seen at dawning
as first I saw you, from shipboard,
by light of moon that challenged morning,
your beauty stood to be adored,
you radiated bridal splendour:
against the sky, pellucid-tender,
your mountains raised their gleaming breasts;
your patchwork of ravines and crests
and trees and hamlets kept unfolding.
And there, in Tartar huts ... what fire,
what sad enchantments of desire,
awoke in me, and soon were holding
my all too ardent bosom fast!
My Muse, you must forget the past.

XVII

Whatever feelings may have smarted
inside me then, they fled away:
they're all transmuted or departed ...

---

* Mithridates, King of Pontus, had himself killed by a slave in 63 B.C. after a long and unsuccessful war with Rome.
† Orestes and his friend Pylades each offered to die in the other's place when captured and condemned to be sacrificed by the high priest of Artemis at the Tauric Chersonese.
‡ A. B. Mickiéwicz: Polish poet and patriot, visited the Crimea in 1825 and composed eighteen *Crimean Sonnets*.

peace to you, storms of yesterday!
Then my imagination ordered
deserts, and billows pearly-bordered,
sea-tumult, summits craggy-browed,
with my ideal, the maiden proud,
and sufferings quite beyond redeeming . . .
and yet new seasons always bring
new visions; humbled is my spring
with its inebriated dreaming,
and, as a poet, I've topped up
the water-quotient in my cup.

XVIII

Today, I'll buy a different ticket:
I like a sandy hillside track,
a hut, two ash-trees and a wicket,
some fencing with a broken back,
a sky where greyish clouds are flying,
a threshing-floor where straw is lying,
and in the shade of willow-trees
a pond where ducklings take their ease;
now balalaikas are my pleasure,
the trepák* with its tipsy clop
outside the village drinking-shop.
I live for quiet, what I treasure
as my ideal is the housewife—
and cabbage soup, and my own life.

XIX

Not long ago, in rainy weather,
I turned into the cattle-yard . . .
Rubbish! Too prosy altogether,

* The trepák: A Russian popular dance.

the Flemish School's diffuse regard!
Was I, when I'd my prime to impel me—
O Bakhchisaray Fountain,* tell me—
as dull as this, or was such trash
suggested by your endless plash
as, silent, instant procreator
of my Zaréma, I stood there?
Those halls, deserted, sumptuous, bare,
Onegin entered three years later,
when, in my wake, he chanced to be
in the same lands, and thought of me.

XX

My home at that time was Odessa
the dusty, whose clear sky prevails,
where an abundant trade's possessor
is ever busy hoisting sails.
There Europe blows on all the breezes,
life glitters with the South, and pleases
as shiftingly its hues unfold.
The speech of Italy, land of gold,
rings in the merry streets, the places
where lordly Slavs and Frenchmen walk,
where Spaniards and Armenians talk,
Moldavians, heaviest of races,
and Greeks, and Egypt's sons are there,
and Moralí, half-pay Corsair.

XXI

Odessa in sonorous fashion
our friend Tumansky† set to rhyme,

---

* *The Fountain of Bakhchisaray:* Poem published by Pushkin in 1824.
† Tumansky: Like Pushkin himself, was on Count Vorontsov's staff in Odessa. He published a poem about Odessa in 1824.

and yet it was with too much passion
that he looked on it at that time.
He arrived, and like a regular poet
took his lorgnette to get to know it,
and roamed the shore alone, and then
Odessa's gardens with his pen
he sang in verses that enchanted.
So far, so good, and yet in fact
all round is steppeland's naked tract;
and only recent toil has planted
young boughs that on dog-days are made
to offer a conscripted shade.

XXII

Where did my rambling story leave you?
Odessa, town of dust, I said.
I well could say, and not deceive you,
Odessa, town of mud, instead.
Five or six weeks, by disposition
of squally Zeus, bring a condition
each year of stoppage and of flood
and foundering-up in thickest mud.
Houses are two feet in, pedestrians
daren't ford the street without a stilt
to take them safely through the silt:
bogged carriages, engulfed equestrians—
from drozhky's shafts poor horse is gone,
and straining ox must carry on.

XXIII

But stones are being hammered, paving
will soon be ringing in the street,
and soon the town will be for saving

as with a base of armoured sheet.
And yet, in waterlogged Odessa,
we still must reckon with no less a
deficiency of—what d'you think?
We're short of water fit to drink.
There's much work to be done ... but really
is it so grave for you and me
when wine's imported customs-free?
And southern sun, and sea ... Ideally
what more could we desire, my friend?
Blest country, fortunate world's end!

XXIV

Hardly from shipboard had exploded
the thunder of the sunrise gun,
than seaward down the steep-eroded
littoral I'd be on the run.
And then, with hookah incandescent,
my thoughts by brine made effervescent,
like Moslems in their paradise
I'd drink, complete with grounds and spice,
an Eastern coffee. Time for walking.
Already open is the blest
Casino; cups are clinked with zest;
on balcony, still tired from chalking,
the marker plies his broom; below
two merchants have just said "hello."

XXV

The square has swarmed. You look about it—
it comes to life; and like a game
they run, on business or without it,

mostly on business all the same.
Offspring of risk and circumspection,
the merchant goes on an inspection
of flags, to see if heaven's consigned
him sails he knows. He wants to find
each cargo that's just been imported
and registered in quarantine.
Has the wine shipment yet been seen?
What plagues, what fires have been reported?
Is there no famine, or no war,
or nothing new like that in store?

XXVI

We, carefree children on the roister
amidst the *affairé* merchants, had
no worry but to await the oyster
brought from the shores of Tsaregrad.*
Oysters? They've just come in. Delicious!
Away the young have flown, lubricious
gourmets, to gulp from the seashells
those plump, live hermits in their cells,
splashed with a drop of lemon. Babel
of argument—and a light wine
that Automne† from his cellar-shrine,
ever obliging, brings to table;
the hours fly past, and the grim bill
invisibly grows grimmer still.

* Tsaregrad: Constantinople.
† César Automne: *Patron* of a restaurant opposite the Casino.

XXVII

But the blue evening's dimmed; no later
it's Opera-time, and off we go
for Rossini, arch-captivator,
Europe's spoilt Orpheus, is on show.
To scowling critics inattentive,
always the same, always inventive,
he pours out melodies that hiss,
that kindle like a youthful kiss,
that flow, that burn, that move and trouble,
all sensuous languor, flaming love,
like Aÿ shooting out above
in fizzing flood and golden bubble . . .
But dare I, gentlemen, d'you think,
equate do-re-mi-sol with drink?

XXVIII

Does that exhaust the fascinations?
Are there no fields for glass to explore?
What about back-stage assignations,
or prima donna, or ballet corps?
The box where, brilliant apparition
compact of languor and ambition,
there sits the merchant's youthful wife,
hemmed by a throng of slaves-for-life?
She listens, heedful yet unheedful,
to cavatinas and to prayers
and jokes and flattery mixed in layers . . .
meanwhile her spouse, out of his needful
nap in a corner, shouts "Encore!"
and yawns—and starts to again snore.

XXIX

Now the finale roars; spectators
forsake the hall in noisy flight;
the square is packed with celebrators
by lantern-light or by starlight;
happy Ausonia's sons are singing
a light, gay aria that keeps ringing
in memory without conscious leave—
while we boom the recitative.
It's late. Odessa's quietly dreaming;
breathless and warm and deeply still
the night. The moon's above the sill,
and a thin veil, pellucid-gleaming,
enfolds the sky. Silence all round;
the Black Sea makes the only sound . . .

XXX

And so I lived then in Odessa . . .

GRAF NULIN

It's time, hurrah! the horns are blaring;
already mounted on their steeds
since dawn, the whippers-in sit wearing
hunt livery; hounds jump their leads.
Up on the *perron* the landowner,
with hands on hips, surveys the scene;
his face is radiant, his persona
is nicely, pompously serene.
His tight-drawn jacket is Caucasian;
at belt, a Turkish knife is worn;
rum in a flask for each occasion,
and, on its chain of bronze, a horn.
In shawl and nightcap, his good wife,
eyes full of sleep, from the window
glares at this whirl of sporting life.
Her husband's horse is set to go;
he grasps the withers with a smack
and, foot in stirrup, stops to call:
"Natasha, don't expect me back!"
then off they gallop, one and all.

September's drawing to a close
(to use the humble tongue of prose);
the country's muddy, nasty, boring;
there's autumn wind, fine snow and rain
and howl of wolves. But oh what roaring
bliss for the sportsman! Out, you vain
comforts! Across the field he prances,
he sleeps at random—hill or plain—
he swears, he drips, he toasts the chances
of his sanguinary campaign.

But how shall his deserted treasure,
while he's away, employ her leisure?
What, has she got no tasks to heed?
Mushrooms to pickle, geese to feed,
orders to give for lunch and dinner,
store-rooms and cellar to inspect.
The housewife's optic—it's a winner;
it spots at once the least defect.
Alas, the heroine of our fable
(oh, I forgot her proper name!
Natasha to her spouse, *our* label,
reader, for her is, I proclaim,
Natalya Pavlovna) had never
given her time up to transact
any domestic jobs whatever;
Natalya Pavlovna in fact
had undergone her early schooling,
not under our traditional ruling,
but at the *pension distinguée*
of Falbala the *émigrée*.

She sits beside the window-sill;
in front of her is open still
the final tome of a four-decker:
"The Loves of Armand and Rebecca,
or The Two Families, a Tale"—
a novel, classic, sentimental,
long as your arm, quite monumental,
old-fashioned, decorous and gentle,
far, far from the romantic trail.

Natalya Pavlovna was reading
her book attentively at first,
but early on in the proceeding,

under her window, an outburst
between a yard-dog and a goat
caught her attention by the throat.
Boys in a mirthful ring stood viewing
as, past her window, gobbling hard,
lugubrious turkeys were pursuing
a sodden rooster round the yard,
and in a pond three ducks were sloshing;
a peasant-woman crossed the slime
towards the fence, to hang up washing;
the weather, spoiling all the time,
suggested snow somewhere about . . .
when, all at once, the bells rang out.

To those who've lived in backwood-places,
my friends, there's no need to expound
how violently the heartbeat races
when first we hear that distant sound.
Could it not be some friend, belated,
from our wild youth? . . . Could it be fated
that it be *she?* . . . My God, it's still
nearer. The heart is wildly beating.
But now the bells go past; retreating,
they die away behind the hill.

Natalya Pavlovna, delighted,
runs to the balcony, full of hope;
she looks: beyond the stream she's sighted
just by the mill, a carriage flying,
it's on the bridge—it's coming *here* . . .
But no, it's turned off left. A tear
starts as she looks, she's all but crying . . .
But suddenly . . . o joy! the slope—
the carriage on its side. "Hi, Vaska!

who's there? be quick! see that *kolyaska*:*
bring it at once into our yard
and ask the master in to sup;
that's, if he's still alive . . . run hard,
find out what's happened—hurry up!"
The obedient servant makes all haste;
Natalya Pavlovna has raced
to find a shawl, fluff her thick hair;
to twitch a curtain, shift a chair;
she waits: how long they take to arrive!
At last, they're coming up the drive.
Mud-stained from its peripatetic
journeying, battered and pathetic,
painfully creeps the *équipage*;
behind it hobbles its young master.
His French valet, despite disaster,
says cheerfully: *"Allons, courage!"*
They're up the steps, and at a crawl
the master's taken to one side,
shown to a room beyond the hall,
with a doorway thrown open wide;
while Picard fusses round, arranging,
his master quite insists on changing;
shall I inform you who he is?
Graf Nulin, coming in a whizz
from foreign countries, where with passion
he's blued his rents on fun and fashion.
To Petropol he's rushing now,
like some strange beast, to make his bow,
with *fracs* and waistcoats in profusion,
hats, buckles, fans and a confusion
of corsets, pins, lorgnettes and smocking

* Carriage.

and every kind of see-through stocking,
with Guizot's latest work—quite shocking—
a sheaf of sharp cartoons he's got
and the new book by Walter Scott,
bons mots from the Parisian Court,
Béranger's songs, and cavatini
both by Paer and by Rossini—
everything you can name, in short.
   The table's set; it's getting late;
the lady's had too long to wait;
now the door opens, here's the Graf;
Natalya Pavlovna, who half-
rises, enquires, in tones polite,
how is he, how's his leg? "All right,"
replies the Count. And now they've passed
into the dining-room, and fast
as light, the Graf's no sooner seated
than he moves up to her his place
and starts to talk: what a disgrace
is Holy Russia! he's defeated—
how can one live in all this snow?
And Paris—what a dreadful show!
"The theatre?" "Hopeless," says the critic.
"C'est bien mauvais, ça fait pitié.
Talma's stone-deaf, and paralytic.
Poor Mamselle Mars has earned her pension.
Of course there's still *le grand* Potier!
By God, Potier alone has been
worthy of honourable mention."
"What writers now get most attention?"
"Still d'Arlincourt and Lamartine."
"Here too they're being imitated."
"Really? so there must be a few
progressive intellects, here too.

May God make Russia educated!"
"And where's the waistline?" "Very low,
almost as far ... I mean, as yet.
Let's take a look at your *toilette*;
so ... *ruches*, ribbons, patterns here:
it's close to fashion, very near."
"You see, we take *The Telegraph*."
"Aha! ... but you must get to know
a splendid vaudeville"—The Graf
begins to sing. "But you don't eat ..."
"I've finished eating ..."

                As they rise
the young hostess has sparkling eyes;
the Count observes to his surprise
(forgetting Paris): she's quite sweet.
The evening passes all unreckoned;
the Graf's *distrait*; the hostess now
talks charmingly, then in a second
her eyes are timidly downcast.
But look—midnight's arrived, somehow.
From the front hall there comes a blast
of snoring; cocks begin to crow;
the watchman beats his iron plating;
the *salon* candles have burnt low.

    Natalya Pavlovna at last
rises: "Good night! our beds are waiting.
Sleep well!" He stands up, quite upset,
our Count, with half-lovelorn regret
kisses her hand. And on my honour
(whatever next?) that wicked tease—
may the good Lord have mercy on her—
silently gives his hand a squeeze.

Natalya Pavlovna's undressing;
in front of her, Parasha waits.
Parasha, there's no need for stressing,
knows all her secrets, calms her states;
she sews, she gossips, and she washes,
begs for old cloaks and old galoshes,
sometimes she humours master's whim,
sometimes she shouts abuse at him,
sometimes she tells Madame a whopper.
Now she discourses, grave and proper,
about the Graf and his affairs,
there's not a detail that she spares—
God knows how she does her exploring.
At length her mistress says: "Who cares?
I've had enough, it's all too boring,"
asks for her nightcap and her gown,
sends off Parasha, and lies down.

Meanwhile the Frenchman too has quite
undressed his master for the night.
The Count lies down, wants a cigar,
soon brought him by Monsieur Picard,
plus silver tumbler, silver crock,
clippers or tweezers with a spring,
bronze candlestick, alarum clock
and uncut novel for last thing.

He lies, and without concentration
he skims a page of Walter Scott.
But he's bemused, our Graf; he's got
a ravaging preoccupation;
he thinks: am I in love or not?
What if I could be? . . . how disarming!
why, it could even be quite charming!

our hostess likes me, there's no doubt—
and Nulin put his candle out.

But feverish distress is keeping
the Count awake—and an unsleeping
devil torments him with a show
of sinful dreams. Our bold hero
pictures his hostess all too clearly,
those eyes that speak out so sincerely,
that rather full and rounded form,
that voice, that womanly inflection,
the country bloom of her complexion,
(what use is rouge, when health's the norm?)
He thinks of a small foot's projection;
he has so clear a recollection
of how her hand pressed his with cool
indifference; no, he's a fool,
he should have stayed, and caught that second
when her capricious humour beckoned—
but still it's not too late. His door
is open now; he's on the floor—
and straight away, across his shoulder
he slings a bright silk dressing gown;
in darkness knocks a chair right down;
seeking the prize that crowns the bolder,
to his Lucretia this Tarquin
sets out, resolved to dare, and win.

Just so at times a cunning house-
tomcat, the servant's mincing pet,
steals from the stove towards a mouse:
slowly he inches, slowlier yet,
he crouches, eyes half-screwed together,
he creeps, his tail sweeps like a feather,

he flashes out a crafty paw
and *tsap!* poor mouse is on the claw.

So through the dark the Graf is creeping,
lovelorn, inflamed with passions leaping;
tentatively he gropes toward
his goal, he hardly breathes, in mortal
terror when under him a board
begins to creak. The sacred portal
is close at hand, without a sound
he squeezes the bronze handle round;
upon its hinge the door is turning;
he looks: the bedroom's dimly lit,
lit by a lamp that's hardly burning;
she lies in slumber deep and sound—
or else she's simply shamming it.

He enters, halts, begins returning—
then all at once kneels at her side.
She ... now I ask you, with permission,
Petersburg ladies, to decide
when, in a terrified condition,
Natalya Pavlovna comes to,
what, in your judgment, she should do.

Opening enormous eyes, she gazes
up at the Count, and our hero
sprays her with standard amorous phrases,
meanwhile a bold hand starts to go
across the quilt, and while it's crawling,
at first she finds her plight appalling ...
then, suddenly returned to sense—
her pride and rage have made her tense—

(also, it may be, frightened), swinging
her arm she caught Tarquin a ringing
smack in the face: yes, all the same,
a smack of smacks, a slap stupendous!

Graf Nulin, quite on fire with shame
before an insult so horrendous—
I find it hard to say how deep
his vengeful fury at this slapping . . .
when shaggy Pom with sudden yapping
disturbed Parasha's heavy sleep.
Graf Nulin heard her footsteps nearing,
and, cursing this ill-omened night
and wilful beauty's fickle veering,
withdrew in ignominious flight.

How hostess, maidservant, and he
got through the night's remaining hours
I leave, without support from me,
to your imaginative powers.

The Count was silent in the morning,
he dressed with indolence, and, yawning,
to trimming of his rosy-nailed
fingers he vaguely then adverted;
carelessly with his tie he flirted,
while his wet comb entirely failed
to smooth those locks so neatly tailed.
What was he thinking? Don't ask me.
But soon they summon him for tea.
What's to be done? The embarrassed Count
with secret fury to surmount
goes as he's asked.

                        The youthful joker,
keeping derisive eyes downcast,
bit scarlet lips, on mediocre
topics talked modestly. There passed
some moments that were slightly paining;
the Graf is rapidly regaining
his confidence, and not above
a half-hour later on, he's smiling,
he's cracking jokes, he's quite beguiling,
once more he's almost back in love.
Then, noise outside, someone's come driving.
"Natasha, hey!"

                    NATALYA PAVLOVNA
                        God, he's arriving.
Count, this is my husband. My sweet:
Count Nulin.

                        HUSBAND
                        Very glad to meet . . .
What absolutely filthy weather!
The smith has got your carriage fit
for you to drive away in it.
Natasha! we ran down a hare
right in the garden over there.
Hey, vodka! Graf, you'll have a drink,
it comes from far away; you'll share
our dinner with us? what d'you think?

                        COUNT
    Well, I don't know, I'm rather pressed . . .

HUSBAND
Count, no objections, you're our guest.
My wife and I love entertaining.
Stay, do!

But with no hope remaining
and deeply disappointed—no,
the Graf insists that he must go.
Groaning, but strengthened by a tincture,
Picard straps the valise's cincture;
two men to the calash have gone
carrying the trunk, and screwed it on.
Round to the front comes the conveyance,
Picard has quickly stowed the bags,*
the Graf drives off ... In such abeyance
this story could conclude, my friends;
but just a word before it ends.

The wife, once lost from sight the carriage,
informed the partner of her marriage
about the exploit of the Graf,
then told the tale to every neighbour ...
Natalya Pavlovna could laugh,
but who laughed loudest? Days of labour
could never help you guess. "Why not?
Her husband?" No, no, no, you've got
it all quite wrong. He was offended
deeply: the Count was a *durák,*†
a milksop, and before it ended
he'd make him howl, by God, he'd track
him down, and hunt him with his pack.

* This line has no answering rhyme in the original.
† Fool.

Lidin it was who laughed, you see,
a neighbour aged just twenty-three . . .

How right we are in emphasising,
as we examine modern life,
my friends, that in a virtuous wife
there's nothing that's at all surprising.

(At the end of 1825.)

MOZART AND SALIERI

Scene One

[A room]

SALIERI

Everyone says, there's no truth in this world;
there's no truth either, even higher up.
This is as plain to me as a simple scale.
Ever since birth, my love has been for art;
I remember, as a child, our ancient church,
on high the organ pealing, and I listened,
listened with all my ears; in spite of me
the sweet tears flowed. And from the earliest age
I shunned all vain enjoyment; any science
that had no link with music, I detested;
I found it hateful—turned my face away
from it in obstinacy and in pride;
music was all my life. But the first step
was hard; the first road, boring. I withstood
the opening trials, I built up craftsmanship
as pedestal for art, became a craftsman;
I taught my fingers a fluency that was
expressionless and docile; trained my ear
to truth. I murdered sounds, and then dissected
music like a cadaver. Harmony
became for me an algebra. It was then
that, tempted out from science, I first dared
to assay the bliss of the creative dream.
Embarked upon creation, but in silence,
in secrecy, I never ventured yet
to think of glory. Often, having sat

two or three days long in my silent cell,
forgetting sleep and food, tasting the joys
and tears of inspiration, I would burn
my handiwork, and coldly watch my thought,
and all the notes I'd given birth to, blaze
and vanish in a thread of smoke! ... But no;
 when the great Gluck appeared, when he revealed
to us new secrets—deep and captivating!—
did I not then abandon all I knew,
all that I'd loved so much, all I believed
so fervently, did I not boldly march
without a murmur after him, just like
a lost wayfarer meeting with someone
who sets him on a different path? At length,
by force of effort and the most intense
perseverance, I reached a high degree
in the frontierless realms of art. And fame
already smiled on me; in people's hearts
I found a chord that echoed my creations.
My life was happy; I enjoyed in peace
labour, success and glory, yes, also
the labour and successes of my friends,
of my companions in the marvellous art.
No, never once did I experience envy!
O, never, never!—neither when Piccini
managed to captivate the boorish ear
of the Parisian, nor when first I heard
the opening phrases of *Iphigenia*.
Who could have forecast that the proud Salieri
would one day change to a contemptible
envier, to a serpent that men crush
as it gnaws feebly at the dust and sand?
No one! ... But now—I'll say the word myself—
I am an envier! ... Yes, I envy deeply

and agonisingly. O God in Heaven!
where's justice, when the consecrated gift,
when genius the immortal is not sent
as prize for blazing love, and self-denial,
labour, and zeal, and prayer, but comes down
to shine upon the forehead of a madman,
a trivial idler? ... Oh, Mozart, Mozart!
                              [Enter Mozart]

MOZART

Ah, so you've seen me! But I had been hoping
to treat you to a joke you didn't expect.

SALIERI

You're here! Since when?

MOZART
                              This minute. On my way,
bringing along something I had to show you,
just as I passed the inn, all of a sudden
I heard a violin ... No, dear Salieri!
Never in all my lifetime have I listened
to anything more comic! ... At the inn
a blind violinist, playing, I swear it's true,
voi che sapete! No, I couldn't wait,
I've brought the fiddler with me, to entertain
you with his art. Come in.
                              [Enter an old man with a violin]
                              Now play something
from Mozart!
                              [The old man plays an aria from
Don Giovanni; Mozart laughs]

SALIERI

And you have the face to laugh?

MOZART

But you, Salieri, aren't you laughing?

SALIERI

No.

To me, nothing's for laughter when a useless
dauber is botching up Raphael's Madonna;
to me, nothing's for laughter, when some base
buffoon in an ignoble parody
degrades the name of Dante. Old man, go!

MOZART

Wait just a minute: here—to drink my health!
                    [The old man goes]
Salieri, you're in a bad mood just now.
I'll come to visit you another time.

SALIERI

What have you brought me?

MOZART

Nothing—just a trifle.

The other night I couldn't sleep; a few
ideas came to me. Today I've sketched them out.
I wanted your opinion; but just now
you're out of humour.

SALIERI

Oh, Mozart, Mozart!

For you, when am I ever out of humour?
Sit down. I'll listen.

MOZART [at the piano]
> Picture to yourself . . .
Who shall it be? me, if you like, but younger;
in love—but not too much, just very slightly;
I'm with a beauty, or a friend—perhaps
with you; I'm cheerful. But then all at once:
a spectacle of death, a sudden darkness,
something of that sort. Listen.
> [He plays]

SALIERI
> And with this
you came to me, then had the strength to stop
in front of the inn, to hear the blind violinist!—
By God, Mozart, you don't deserve yourself.

MOZART
What, is it good?

SALIERI
> Such boldness! such profundity!
and such proportion! Mozart, you're a god;
you don't know it yourself—it's I who know!

MOZART
Bah! could that be the truth? Well, I suppose . . .
But my godhead is starving.

SALIERI
> Listen, we
could go together to the Golden Lion.

MOZART

By all means. I'd be delighted. Give me time
just to go home and tell my wife she's not
to expect me there for dinner.   [He goes]

SALIERI
                                    I'll wait here;
be sure you come!
                        No, I can't fight my fate:
I've been picked out to stop him, otherwise
we'll all be ruined, music's priests, its servants,
not I alone, with my dull reputation . . .
No, what use is it, if Mozart lives on
and reaches a new summit? by so doing
will he raise art up higher? No! as soon
as he is gone, it will sink down again:
he leaves no heir behind him. So whatever
use can he be? Just like some cherubim,
he's brought us a few songs of paradise,
only to rouse in us wingless desires,
a smoke of dust—and then to fly away!
Then off you fly! the sooner so, the better!
                        Here is a poison, my Isaure's last gift.
For eighteen years I've carried it with me;
often my life meanwhile has seemed a wound
too painful to be borne; often I've sat
at the same table with some unconcerned
enemy and never yielded to temptation's
whispered address, although I'm not a coward,
however deeply I may feel affronts,
however little I may value life.
Yet I delayed, although a thirst for death
tormented me—why die? I thought, perhaps
life may yet bring me unpredicted gifts;

perhaps delight will come, and a creative
midnight, and inspiration; or perhaps
another Haydn will create some marvel
for my enchantment . . . so as I sat feasting
with my unlovely guest, I thought, one day
perhaps I'll find a mortal enemy;
perhaps some mortal outrage will project me
headlong from pride's high mountain—ah, but then
you won't desert me, gift of my Isaure.
And I was right! I have both found at last
my enemy, and have been quite transported
with wonder and delight by a new Haydn!
Yes, now it's time. You hallowed gift of love,
you must this day pass into friendship's cup.

Scene Two

[A private room in an inn: a piano]
Mozart and Salieri at table.

SALIERI

Why so cast down today?

MOZART

I? No.

SALIERI

Mozart,
I'm certain that there's something which disturbs you.
The dinner's good, and there's a glorious wine,
yet you sit silent, scowling . . .

MOZART

                         I admit it,
I'm worried by my Requiem.

SALIERI

                         So it's
a Requiem you've been writing. For some time?

MOZART

Oh, yes a good three weeks. But something strange . . .
Have I not told you?

SALIERI
Never.

MOZART

                         Well, just listen:
three weeks ago, I came home late. They said
someone had called for me. Why, I don't know,
but all night long I wondered who it was
and what he wanted from me? The next day
he called again, again he found me absent.
The third day I was playing on the floor
with my small lad. They called me; I went out.
A man, dressed all in black, bowed deeply to me,
commissioned me to write a Requiem and
vanished. So I at once sat down and started
to write—and since that day my man in black
has not returned; but I've been glad: it would
have been a sorrow to be parted from
my Requiem, although by now it's quite
ready and finished. But meanwhile I . . .

SALIERI
What?

MOZART
I'm quite ashamed to admit it . . .

SALIERI
To admit what?

MOZART
My man in black, by day or night he gives me
no minute's peace. He trails me everywhere
just like a shadow. Even now I think
he's sitting here between us.

SALIERI
No, enough!
What childish terrors! You must chase away
such idle thoughts. Beaumarchais said to me:
"listen, my dear Salieri, when ideas
of gloom attack you, then uncork champagne
or else re-read *The Marriage of Figaro*."

MOZART
Well, yes! Beaumarchais was of course your friend;
it was for him that you composed *Tarara*,
that glorious work. There's a motif in it . . .
when I feel happy, I sing it constantly . . .
La la la la . . . But is it true, Salieri,
that Beaumarchais once poisoned someone?

SALIERI
No,
I doubt it; he was too much of a joker
for such a trade.

MOZART
                    In fact he was a genius
like you and me. Genius and villainy
don't go together, do they?

            SALIERI
                    Don't you think so?
                    [He drops poison in Mozart's glass]
Well, drink.

            MOZART
            Here's to your health, my friend,
to the true link uniting Mozart and
Salieri, those two sons of harmony.
                    [He drinks]

            SALIERI
But wait, but wait! . . . you've drunk alone . . . without me?

                    MOZART [throws his napkin on the table]
Enough, I've finished.   [He goes to the piano]
                    Now, Salieri, listen,
my Requiem . . . [He plays]
                    You're weeping?

            SALIERI
                        Yes, these tears
are the first ones I've shed: there's pain, there's pleasure,
as if I'd carried out some heavy task,
as if some salutary knife had severed
an ailing member! Dear Mozart, these tears . . .
don't notice them. Continue, hurry on,
pour still more sounds into my soul . . .

MOZART

If only

everybody could so feel the strength
of harmony! But no: for in that case
the world could not continue: no one would
trouble about life's grosser cares—and all
would dedicate themselves to untrammeled art!
How few of us there are, we happy idlers,
we chosen ones who spurn the ignoble call
of mere utility, priests dedicated
only to beauty. But just now I feel
a sickness, something weighing heavy on me;
I'll go and sleep. Farewell.

SALIERI

Till our next meeting.

[Alone]

Yes, go to your long sleep, Mozart! . . .

But was he

not right? and am I not a genius too?
Genius and villainy don't go together.
That's wrong: take Buonarrotti?* . . . Or is that
a fable of the thoughtless herd—and was
the Vatican's creator no assassin?

(26 October 1830)

* This refers to the allegation that Michelangelo killed the sculptor Torri-
giano in a drunken brawl.

THE BRONZE HORSEMAN

A Petersburg Tale

FOREWORD

The event described in this tale is based on fact. The details of the flood are borrowed from newspapers of the time. The curious can consult the account compiled by V. I. Berkh.

INTRODUCTION

Upon the brink of the wild stream
He stood, and dreamt a mighty dream.
He gazed far off. Near him the spreading
river poured by; with flood abeam,
alone, a flimsy skiff was treading.
Scattered along those shores of bog
and moss were huts of blackened log,
the wretched fisher's squalid dwelling;
forests, impervious in the fog
to hidden suns, all round were telling
their whispered tale.
                      And so thought He:
"From here, proud Sweden will get warning;
just here is where a city'll be
founded to stop our foes from scorning;
here Nature destines us to throw
out over Europe a window;*

---

* Algarotti said somewhere: *"Petersbourg est la fenêtre, par laquelle la Russie regarde en Europe."* (*Pushkin's note.*)

to stand steadfast beside the waters;
across waves unknown to the West,
all flags will come, to be our guest—
and we shall feast in spacious quarters."
   A century went by—a young
city, of Northern lands the glory
and pride, from marsh and overhung
forest arose, storey on storey:
where, earlier, Finland's fisher sank—
of Nature's brood the most downhearted—
alone on the low-lying bank,
his ropy net in the uncharted
current, today, on brinks that hum
with life and movement, there have come
enormous mansions that are justling
with graceful towers; and vessels here
from earth's extremities will steer
until the rich quayside is bustling.
Nevá now sports a granite face;
bridges are strung across her waters;
in darkly verdant garden-quarters
her isles have vanished without trace;
old Moscow's paled before this other
metropolis; it's just the same
as when a widowed Empress-Mother
bows to a young Tsaritsa's claim.
   I love you, Peter's own creation;
I love your stern, your stately air,
Nevá's majestical pulsation,
the granite that her quaysides wear,
your railings with their iron shimmer,
your pensive nights in the half-gloom,
translucent twilight, moonless glimmer,
when, sitting lampless in my room,

I write and read; when, faintly shining,
the streets in their immense outlining
are empty, given up to dreams;
when Admiralty's needle gleams;
when not admitting shades infernal
into the golden sky, one glow
succeeds another, and nocturnal
tenure has one half-hour to go;
I love your brutal winter, freezing
the air to so much windless space;
by broad Nevá the sledges breezing;
brighter than roses each girl's face;
the ball, its brilliance, din, and malice;
bachelor banquets and the due
hiss of the overflowing chalice,
and punch's radiance burning blue.
I love it when some warlike duty
livens the Field of Mars, and horse
and foot impose on that concourse
their monolithic brand of beauty;
above the smooth-swaying vanguard
victorious, tattered flags are streaming,
on brazen helmets light is gleaming,
helmets that war has pierced and scarred.
I love the martial detonation,
the citadel in smoke and roar,
when the North's Empress to the nation
has given a son for empire, or
when there's some new triumph in war
victorious Russia's celebrating;
or when Nevá breaks the blue ice,
sweeps it to seaward, slice on slice,
and smells that days of spring are waiting.
    Metropolis of Peter, stand,

steadfast as Russia, stand in splendour!
Even the elements by your hand
have been subdued and made surrender;
let Finland's waves forget the band
of hate and bondage down the ages,
nor trouble with their fruitless rages
Peter the Great's eternal sleep!
    A fearful time there was: I keep
its memory fresh in retrospection . . .
My friends, let me turn up for you
the dossiers of recollection.
Grievous the tale will be, it's true . . .

(29 October)

PART ONE

    On Petrograd, the darkened city,
November, chill and without pity,
blasted; against its noble brink
Nevá was splashing noisy billows;
its restless mood would make one think
of sufferers on their restless pillows.
The hour was late and dark; the rain
angrily lashed the window-pane,
the wind blew, pitifully shrieking.
From house of friends, about this time,
young Evgeny came home . . .
                        My rhyme
selects this name to use in speaking
of our young hero. It's a sound
I like; my pen has long been bound
in some way with it; further naming
is not required, though lustre flaming

in years gone by might have lit on
his forebears, and perhaps their story
under Karamzin's pen had shone,
resounding to the nation's glory;
but now by all, both high and low,
it's quite forgotten. Our hero
lives in Kolomna, has employment
in some bureau, tastes no enjoyment
of wealth or fashion's world, and no
regret for tales of long ago.

So Evgeny came home and, shaking
his greatcoat, got undressed for bed—
but lay long hours awake, his head
with various thoughts disturbed and aching.
What did he think about? The fact
that he was penniless; that packed
mountains of work must be surmounted
to earn him freedom, fame, and ease;
that wit and money might be counted
to him from God; and that one sees
fellows on permanent vacation,
dull-witted, idle, in whose station
life runs as smooth as in a dream;
that he'd served two years altogether . . .
And he thought also that the weather
had got no gentler; that the stream
was rising, ever higher lifting;
that soon the bridges might be shifting;
that maybe from Parasha he
would be cut off, two days or three.

These were his dreams. And a great sadness
came over him that night; he wished
the raindrops with less raging madness

would lash the glass, that the wind swished
less drearily . . .

At last his failing
eyes closed in sleep. But look, the gloom
of that foul-weather night is paling,
and a weak daylight fills the room . . .
A dreadful day it was!
All night
Nevá against the gales to seaward
had battled, but been blown to leeward
by their ungovernable might . . .*
That morning, on the quayside, fountains
of spray held an admiring crowd,
that pressed to watch the watery mountains,
the foaming waves that roared so loud.
But now, blocked by the headwinds blowing
in from the Gulf, Nevá turned back,
in sullen, thunderous fury flowing,
and flooded all the islands; black,
still blacker grew the day; still swelling,
Nevá exploded, raging, yelling,
in kettle-like outbursts of steam—
until, mad as a beast, the stream
pounced on the city. From its path
everyone fled, and all around
was sudden desert . . . At a bound
cellars were under inundation,
canals leapt rails, forgot their station—
and Triton-Petropol surfaced

* Mickiéwicz described in beautiful verses the day preceding the Petersburg
flood (in one of his best poems, *Oleszkiewicz*). The only pity is that this de-
scription is not accurate; there was no snow, and the Nevá was not covered
with ice. Our description is more faithful, although it lacks the bright col-
ouring of the Polish poet. (*Pushkin's note.*)

with waters lapping round his waist.
    Siege and assault! The waves, malicious,
like thieves, burst in through windows; vicious
rowboats, careering, smash the panes;
stalls are engulfed; piteous remains,
débris of cabins, roofing, boarding,
wares that a thrifty trade's been hoarding,
poor household goods, dashed all astray,
bridges the storm has snatched away,
and scooped-up coffins, helter-skelter
swim down the streets!
             All sense alike
God's wrath, and wait for doom to strike.
Everything's ruined: bread and shelter!
and where to find them?
             That deathlike,
that frightful year, Tsar Alexander
still ruled in glory. He came out
on the balcony, in grief, in doubt,
and said: "A Tsar is no commander
against God's elements." Deep in thought
he gazed with sorrow and confusion,
gazed at the wreck the floods had wrought.
The city squares gave the illusion
of lakes kept brimming to profusion
by torrent-streets. The palace stood
sad as an island in the ocean.
And then the Tsar spoke out, for good
or evil set in farflung motion
his generals on their dangerous way
along those streets of boisterous waters
to save the people in their quarters,
drowning, unhinged by terror's sway.
    And then in Peter's square, where lately

a corner-mansion rose, and stately
from its high porch, on either side,
caught as in life, with paws suspended,
two lions, sentry-like, attended—
perched up on one, as if to ride,
arms folded, motionless, astride,
hatless, and pale with apprehension,
Evgeny sat. His fear's intention
not for himself, he never knew
just how the greedy waters grew,
how at his boots the waves were sucking,
how in his face the raindrops flew;
or how the stormwind, howling, bucking,
had snatched his hat away. His view
was fixed in darkest desperation,
immobile, on a single spot.
Mountainous, from the perturbation
down in the depths, the waves had got
on their high horses, raging, pouncing;
the gale blew up, and, with it, bouncing
wreckage . . . Oh, God, oh God! for there—
close to the seashore—almost where
the Gulf ran in, right on the billow—
a fence, untouched by paint, a willow,
a flimsy cottage; *there* were they,
a widow and his dream, her daughter,
Parasha . . . or perhaps he may
have dreamt it all? Fickle as water,
our life is as dreamlike as smoke—
at our expense, fate's private joke.
As if by sorcery enchanted,
high on the marble fixed and planted,
he can't dismount! And all about
is only water. Looking out,

with back turned to him, on the retching
waves of Nevá in their wild course
from his fast summit, arm outstretching,
the Giant rides on his bronze horse.

(30 October)

PART TWO

But by now, tired of helter-skelter
ruin and sheer rampaging, back
Nevá was flowing, in its track
admiring its own hideous welter;
its booty, as it made for shelter,
it slung away. With his grim crew
so any robber chief will do;
bursting his way into a village,
he'll hack and thrust and snatch and pillage;
rape, havoc, terror, howl and wail!
Then, loaded down with loot, and weary—
fear of pursuers makes them leery—
the robbers take the homeward trail
and as they flee they scatter plunder.
So, while the waters fell asunder,
the road came up. And fainting, pale,
in hope and yearning, fear and wonder,
Evgeny hurries at full steam
down to the scarcely falling stream.
And yet, still proud, and still exulting,
the waves, still furious and insulting,
boiled as if over flames alight;
they still were lathered, foaming, seething
and deeply the Nevá was breathing
just like a horse flown from a fight.

Evgeny looks: a skiff is waiting—
Godsent—he rushes, invocating
the ferryman, who without a care
for just a few copecks quite gladly
agrees to take him, though still madly
the floods are boiling everywhere.
The boatman fought the agonising
billows like an experienced hand;
the cockboat with its enterprising
crew was quite ready for capsizing
at any moment—but dry land
at last it gained.
                    Evgeny, tearful,
rushes along the well-known ways
towards the well-known scene. His gaze
finds nothing it can grasp: too fearful
the sight! before him all is drowned,
or swept away, or tossed around;
cottages are askew, some crumbled
to sheer destruction, others tumbled
off by the waves; and all about,
as on a field of martial rout,
bodies lie weltered. Blankly staring,
Evgeny, uncomprehending, flies,
faint from a torment past all bearing,
runs to where fate will meet his eyes,
fate whose unknown adjudication
still waits as under seal of wax.
And now he's near his destination
and here's the Gulf, here . . . in his tracks
Evgeny halts . . . the house . . . where ever?
he goes back, he returns. He'd never . . .
he looks . . . he walks . . . he looks again:
here's where their cottage stood; and then

here was the willow. Gates were standing
just here—swept off, for sure. But where's
the cottage gone? Not understanding,
he walked round, full of boding cares,
he talked to himself loud and gruffly,
and then he struck his forehead roughly
and laughed and laughed.
                                In deepest night
the city trembled at its plight:
long time that day's events were keeping
the citizenry all unsleeping
as they rehearsed them.
                                Daylight's ray
fell out of tired, pale clouds to play
over a scene of calm—at dawning
yesterday's hell had left no trace.
The purple radiance of the morning
had covered up the dire event.
All in its previous order went.
Upon highways no longer flowing,
people as everyday were going
in cold indifference, and the clerk
left where he'd sheltered in the dark
and went to work. The daring bosses
of commerce, unperturbed, explore
Nevá's inroads upon their store,
and plan to take their heavy losses
out on their neighbour. From backyards
boats are removed.
                                That bard of bards,
Count Khvostov, great poetic master,
begins to sing Nevá's disaster
in unforgettable ballades.
    But spare, I pray you, spare some pity

for my poor, poor Evgeny, who
by the sad happenings in the city
had wits unhinged. Still the halloo
of tempest and Nevá was shrieking
into his ear; pierced through and through
by frightful thoughts, he roamed unspeaking;
some nightmare held him in its thrall.
A week went by, a month—and all
the time he never once was seeking
his home. That small deserted nook,
its lease expired, his landlord took
for a poor poet. His possessions
Evgeny never went to claim.
Soon to the world and its professions
a stranger, all day long he came
and went on foot, slept by the water;
scraps thrown from windows of the quarter
his only food; always the same,
his clothes wore out to shreds. Malicious
children would stone him; he received
from time to time the coachman's vicious
whiplash, for he no more perceived
which way was which, or what direction
led where; he never seemed to know
where he was going, he was so
plunged in tumult of introspection.
And so his life's unhappy span
he eked out—neither beast nor man—
not this, nor that—not really living
nor yet a ghost . . .
                                He slept one night
by the Nevá. Summer was giving
its place to autumn. Full of spite,
a bad wind blew. In mournful fight

. against the embankment, waves were splashing,
their crests on the smooth steps were smashing
for all the world like suppliant poor
at some hard-hearted judge's door.
Evgeny woke. Raindrops were falling
in midnight gloom; the wind was calling
piteously—on it, far off, hark,
the cry of sentries in the dark . . .
Evgeny rose, and recollection
brought up past horrors for inspection;
he stood in haste, walked off from there,
then halted, and began to stare
in silence, with an insensately
wild look of terror on his face.
He was beside the pillared, stately
front of a mansion. In their place,
caught as in life, with paws suspended,
two lions, sentry-like, attended,
and there, above the river's course,
atop his rock, fenced-off, defended
on his dark summit, arm extended,
the Idol rode on his bronze horse.*

Evgeny shuddered. Thoughts were hatching
in frightful clarity. He knew
that spot, where floods ran raging through—
where waves had massed, voracious, snatching,
a riot-mob, vindictive, grim—
the lions, and the square, and him
who, motionless and without pity,
lifted his bronze head in the gloom,
whose will, implacable as doom,

* See the description of the monument in Mickiéwicz. It is borrowed from
Ruban, as Mickiéwicz himself observes. (*Pushkin's note.*)

had chosen seashore for his city.
Fearful he looked in that half-light!
Upon his forehead, what a might
of thought, what strength of concentration!
what fire, what passion, and what force
are all compact in that proud horse!
He gallops—to what destination?
On the cliff-edge, O lord of fate,
was it not you, O giant idol,
who, pulling on your iron bridle,
checked Russia, made her rear up straight?

Around the hero's plinth of granite
wretched Evgeny, in a daze,
wandered, and turned a savage gaze
on the autocrat of half the planet.
A steely pressure gripped his chest.
His brow on the cold railing pressed,
over his eyes a mist was lowering,
and through his heart there ran a flame;
his blood was seething; so he came
to stand before the overpowering
image, with teeth and fists again
clenched as if some dark force possessed him.
"Take care," he whisperingly addressed him,
"you marvel-working builder, when . . ."
He shivered with bitter fury, then
took headlong flight. He had the impression
that the grim Tsar, in sudden race
of blazing anger, turned his face
quietly and without expression . . .
and through the empty square he runs,
but hears behind him, loud as guns
or thunderclap's reverberation,

ponderous hooves in detonation
along the shuddering roadway—
as, lighted by the pale moon-ray,
one arm stretched up, on headlong course,
after him gallops the Bronze Rider,
after him clatters the Bronze Horse.
So all night long, demented strider,
wherever he might turn his head—
everywhere gallops the Bronze Rider
pursuing him with thunderous tread.
  And from then on, if he was chancing
at any time to cross that square,
a look of wild distress came glancing
across his features; he would there
press hand to heart, in tearing hurry,
as if to chase away a worry;
take his worn cap off; never raise
up from the ground his distraught gaze,
but sidle off.

                   A small isle rises
close to the foreshore. Now and then,
a fisher moors alongside, when
late from his catch, with nets and prizes,
and cooks his poor meal on the sand;
or some official comes to land,
out for a Sunday's pleasure-boating,
on the wild islet. Not a blade
of grass is seen. There, gaily floating,
the floods had washed up as they played
a flimsy cottage. Above water
it showed up like a bush, all black—
last spring they moved it. The small quarter,
empty, was shipped away, all rack

and ruin. Near it, my dim-witted
my mad Evgeny there they found . . .
His cold corpse in that self-same ground
to God's good mercy they committed.

(31 October 1833: Boldino, 5 past 5)

THE TAMBOV LADY

Gamble, but don't try to recoup.
Proverb

DEDICATION

So I'm a Diehard. No displeasure
at such repute—in fact I smile:
I'm writing to Onegin's measure;
I sing, my friends, in olden style.
Listen, I beg you, to this fable—
and it may be that you'll feel able
to approve its unexpected, odd
dénouement with the faintest nod.
In keeping with the old tradition,
we'll lubricate each awkward line
with restorative draughts of wine,
and send it hobbling on its mission
to join its mates by Lethe's stream
in the repose which knows no dream.

I

On the cartographer's projection
Tambov is seldom ringed in red;
once in disgrace through disaffection,
now it's a splendid town instead!
The three straight streets are quite inviting,
complete with pavement and with lighting;
two taverns, one the Moscow Inn,
the other one called The Berlin;
and in their boxes, posed correctly,
two gendarmes keep a twelve-hour spell

of duty, and their job as well
is giving the salute correctly;
*the prison is the place's crown** ...
In short, Tambov's a splendid town.

II

But, God, the boredom! My arraignment
is that, just as on Nevá's strand,[†]
it drugs with dreary entertainment,
caresses with a rasping hand.
Here, too, are socialites disdainful,
and pedants who are something painful;
here, too, you'll find no hideaway
from fools, or musical *soirées*;
here, ladies, too, deserve their laurel:
strict, bonneted Dianas who
say "no" to all, including you.
In front of them, forget immoral
fancies: they *read* a sinful look,
and damn you all with bell and book.

III

One day, to galvanise the gentry,
and put the girls in a ferment,
came news: they could expect the entry,
soon, of a Lancer regiment

* Passages printed in italics in the translation are probably later additions
to Lermontov's text, representing an attempt to reconstruct original lines
deleted by censor or editor. See Introduction, page xvii.
† In St. Petersburg.

to winter in Tambov. Oh, Lancers!
Such dashing fellows, and such dancers! . . .
The Colonel's sure to be unwed;
the General—so the assumption spread—
has planned a brilliant ball. The mothers
have sparkling eyes; those stingy bears,
the fathers, have acquired fresh cares:
sabres and spurs—a plague for others,
the scourge of every painted floor . . .
So all Tambov was in a roar.

IV

Then, at that early hour of morning
when young girls' sleep is most intense,
when, scarcely touched by gleam of dawning,
the Tsna* peers from its shroud so dense,
when the cathedral domes are lightly
brushed with Aurora's gold, when rightly
that well-known plague, that noisy pest,
the drinking-shop is still at rest:
the Lancers, riding six abreast,†
entered the city; their musicians†
sleepily in the saddle swayed—
the Blind Men's March‡ was what they played.

V

To hear the whinnying of black horses
that symphony so long desired—
that's when the heart more swiftly courses,

---

* River on which Tambov stands.
† Line with no rhyming counterpart in the original.
‡ From the opera *Two Blind Men of Toledo* by Étienne Méhul (1763–1817).

that's when the blood's more fiercely fired!
Warm feather-beds are quite forgotten ...
"Malashka, idiot, misbegotten!
Fetch me my slippers and my gown!
And where's Iván? That silly clown!
he takes two years to part a shutter ..."
But now it's open; while they pass,
all hands are rubbing dirty glass—
and maidens' curious glances flutter
from swollen eyelids, to espy
stern dusty faces riding by.

VI

"Cousin, look here ... proud as a Rajah—
d'you see?" "The Major?" "Oh, no, no!
He's handsome—what a splendid charger!
I think he's just a Cornet, though ...
His swagger's quite beyond conceiving ...
I dreamt of him—it's past believing ...
and after that, I couldn't sleep ..."
Then, on a maiden's bosom deep,
the kerchief gently falls and rises,
and a nuance of reverie plays
across the brightness of a gaze.
The regiment's passed. All different sizes,
after it scurry the street-boys,
bare-foot, unwashed, and full of noise.

VII

Across from the Hotel Moskovsky—
that haunt of whiskered raffishness—
there lived a greybeard named Bobkovsky,

the District Treasurer, no less.
His was an oldish habitation,
peaceful and without affectation;
a brace of peeling columns there
propped up a balcony in the air.
The splintered roof was quite a beauty,
with greenest moss all overgrown,
and four trimmed birches grew alone
outside the windows, doing duty
for curtains and for sumptuous blinds—
the coquetry of harmless minds.

VIII

This greybeard, gloomy past all measure—
huge head as hairless as a stone—
long years with the official treasure
had lived as if it were his own.
In sombre realms of calculation
to rove—his chosen occupation;
he gambled too, to be precise—
it was his one and only vice.
On winter nights his loved employment
was dealing right and left, and then
doubling his stake, doubling again,
and punting with supreme enjoyment;
when cards turned sour, he'd not resign
but drown them in Tsimlyansky wine.

IX

He was the foe of useful labours,
tribune of Tambov's sportsman-kind,
bogy to mothers of young neighbours,

but, to their sons, a master-mind.
Quite often, his marked cards were screwing
the harmless revenues accruing
from turkeys, butter, oats and maize—
in half an hour they'd gone their ways.
Three—Doctor, Judge, Police Inspector—
these were his customary group;
the last-named joker, over soup,
told tales that showed him no respecter
of taste; his humour, when it came,
made Mrs. Treasurer blush for shame.

X

So far, I've not expatiated
about my Treasurer's private life.
The good Lord had remunerated
him with a jewel of a wife.
He recognised her value keenly,
and yet he kept her pretty meanly—
no bonnets came, for her to show,
from Petersburg or from Moscow.
He'd taught her an exclusive science:
to shoot a dim glance, or a sigh,
so that no lovelorn punter's eye
should catch him in his skill's appliance—
but the old man was no neophyte:
he wouldn't trust her out of sight.

XI

Luscious Avdotya! her attraction
was of a cast that's rarely found:
she walked with a proud, swimming action—

her slippers hardly touched the ground.
So full, so high a breast had never
been known, at any time whatever,
in Tambov: sugar-white—and plain
to see in it was every vein.
You'd think that for the tender passion
she'd been created. But her eyes . . .
Well, what is turquoise? what are skies?
Anyhow I, in my own fashion
being a blue-eye-devotee,
am not impartial, as you see.

XII

That little nose! those lips—for brightness
as fresh as rose-petals they seem!
Mother-of-pearl her teeth for whiteness,
her voice as sweet as in a dream!
She lisped. To put the point succinctly,
her "r" was not pronounced distinctly;
but who could not forgive in her
this minute fault, this tiny slur?
Her ageing husband with affection
would pat her cheeks. But that they had
no children—this was really sad!
The reason's secret, past detection;
in Tambov, though, there's a supply
of gossips; we could ask them why.

XIII

To unfold my tale in lucid fashion,
it's time for me to tell the worst:
of Dunya's* sister, and the passion
that for a Lancer she had nursed . . .
In manner duly confidential
she had told Dunya this essential.
But have you ever overheard
how married sisters talk? My word,
there's nothing in or out of season
that those delightful lips don't touch!
O Russian frankness, it's too much!
I'm a broad-minded man of reason—
but, unobserved, I've once or twice
overheard what was hardly nice . . .

XIV

And so, by now, my Tambov beauty†
knew how to value a moustache† . . .
What then? the knowledge was her ruin!
A Lancer would be her undoing.
A charming rake (I knew him well)
had got a room in the hotel
that faced the room she used for dressing.
He was some thirty summers old;
a junior Captain, but his mould
slim as a Cornet's; prepossessing
dark whiskers, flashing Russian eyes—
the type young girls idealise.

* Familiar form of Avdotya.
† Line with no rhyming counterpart in the original.

XV

While still a Cornet, he had squandered
his heritage; he'd had to live
since then from hand to mouth; he'd wandered,
taking, like birds, what God would to give.
He slept untroubled, never hurried,
for next day's dinner never worried.
Round Russia went his roving course,
in courier-coaches, or to horse,
a remount-officer, half-pickled,
or a philanderer on leave—
exploits too curious to believe,
about which even I'd have stickled
had it not been that all his most
surprising tales were free from boast.

XVI

In him no mundane passions bubbled,
he never tripped, or lost his way.
Heaven would have found him quite untroubled
should he have landed there one day.
Sometimes, perhaps in heat of battle,
he'd raise a laugh by pompous prattle,
by a grimace, by hamming it,
or by some flash of genuine wit.
In joke one day, after a wrangle,
he shot a comrade in the head;
in joke, he too would go for dead
*to save a rogue from the triangle,**

---

* Literally: from the knout.

at times quite gentle, like a child,
and good, and true—but joker-wild.

XVII

A lady's man—that he was never,
in the true meaning of the phrase;
he shunned the beaten path, was ever
expert at paving his own ways.
He shirked all amorous declaration,
he never knelt in supplication:
and yet he was, when it all ends,
luckier than you or I, my friends.*
Such then was junior Captain Garin:
at least the portrait here on show
was accurate five years ago.

XVIII

The landlord briefed him, without losing
a second, on Tambov's affairs.
He learnt of much that was amusing—
of five or six clandestine pairs;
of the headquarters for matchmaking,
of what rich brides were there for taking,
but one disclosure more than all
detained his restless mind in thrall:
it was the plight of his young neighbour.
"Poor wretched girl," the Lancer said:
"that that lethargic old blockhead
can keep you sentenced to hard labour—
shall I, a knave who should be shot,
have no compassion for your lot?"

* Three lines missing.

XIX

Quickly he's at the window, cloaking
his form in Persia's *arkhalouk*:
discreetly in his mouth is smoking
a decoratively carved *chibouk*.
On top of his soft curls he's wearing
a cherry-tinted tarboush, bearing
a golden tassel and thick braid—
the gift of a Moldavian maid.
He sits and watches, all attention . . .
when suddenly, through mist, behind
the window filmily outlined,
looms an angelic head's dimension;
and look, the window from inside
is pushed, and look, it opens wide.

XX

The town is still asleep, and waiting
till, over glass, dawn's glimmer steals,
and from the highway percolating
there's still no sound of carriage wheels . . .
What can so early have awoken
the Treasurer's wife? what, truly spoken,
can be the cause? Perhaps that she
has got insomnia, could it be? . . .
Anyway, head on hand she's sitting;
she sighs, she holds a stocking—no:
stockings aren't really *à propos*—
to talk of them would be unfitting . . .
no, when you come to think of it,
would it be *right* for her to knit?

XXI

Her charming gaze through the celestial
azure was roving, then it came
down to examine things terrestrial,
and suddenly—disgrace and shame!
There, sitting in the window's cavern,
a man in undress, in the tavern!
Quick, junior Captain, your frock-coat!
The window bangs . . . the anecdote
is over; lost, the sweet illusion.
I know what outcome would have had
for you, dear friends, a scene so sad;
it would have caused you deep confusion;
the Lancer, though—give him his due—
said: "As a first step, that'll do."

XXII

Two days the glass stayed shut up tightly;
but he was patient. On the third
once more, behind the window, whitely
a captivating shadow stirred.
The frame squeaked softly; with her knitting
there, at the window, she was sitting.
But the experienced eye could spot
a well-prepared turn-out. So, not
dissatisfied with his achievement,
Garin stood up, and went away,
and never came back till next day.
Then, though it hurt like a bereavement,
he called up all that made him strong:
forsook the window three days long.

XXIII

This sort of tender confrontation
had the effect that they all do:
between the pair a conversation,
distinct, though silent, quickly grew.
Language of love, o language splendid:
by youth alone you're comprehended!
What lover who has ever sung
has not found you his native tongue?
Who, at a time of blazing passion,
has not had you as his helpmeet
by loved one's lips, at loved one's feet?
And whom, beneath the yoke of fashion,
in envious throngs, where hate is rife,
have you not saved by breathing life?

XXIV

In short, within two weeks, for certain
our Garin has contrived to know
what time of day she'll draw her curtain,
drink tea with her consort, and go
out walking, or to holy duty—
to church then he pursues his beauty;
against a pillar, his outline—
he never makes the cross' sign;
a crimson lantern-glimmer dances
over his face: seen by those gleams,
how sombre and how cold it seems!
But his exploratory glances,
now dimmed, now flashing, to her dart—
they seek to penetrate her heart!

XXV

It's long been known—forgive digression—
how curious the fair sex is.
Garin had made a deep impression
upon the Treasurer's wife by his
strangeness of temper. Not that, truly,
she should have licensed thoughts unruly
within her heart to make their way,
and hold their fearsome, fondling sway!*
But loveless life can be so dreary;
what passions can a woman share
with a consort who's got white hair?

XXVI

But days went past, "Time I was coping,"
observed my lover. "As we know,
novels are full of silent moping—
but I'm no story-book hero."
A footman with deep salutation
enters, and hands an invitation.
"My master's compliments to you;
he couldn't come—too much to do—
but home for dinner you're invited,
for dancing too, this evening; he
in person so instructed me."
"Well, go and say I'll be delighted."
At three, well-tunicked and pelissed,
the Captain hastens to the feast.

* Three lines missing.

XXVII

Amphitryon* was the Nobles' Marshal—
and for his spouse's birthday ball—
of custom a severe, impartial
upholder—he'd invited all
the regiment, and the top-rating
locals. The General kept them waiting,
then yawned his head off, but the feast
by this was not spoilt in the least;
it all was ordered very nicely:
huge urns along each table stand
with apples for the ladies, and
the sideboard groans, since dawn precisely,
with three enormous crates of wine
to assist the gentlemen to dine.

XXVIII

Ahead, the host went in to table,
the General's lady on his arm.
So far from men as it was able,
the sex of shyness and of charm
sat down ... And from aloft, to shatter
briefly the reassuring clatter
which spoons and knives and platters made,
the Lancers' trumpet-chorus brayed.
An ancient but enchanting fashion:
while whetting appetite, it may
entirely drown, and hide away,
the dialogue of secret passion;
and yet our moderns know the score:
everything old's a clownish bore.

* Fabulous host, in mythology, and Molière.

XXIX

Today you won't find a suspicion
of the ancient world of the boyars,
except when trumpets of tradition
thunder at banquets of Hussars.
Oh, that I could once more be sitting
among dear comrades—as befitting,
in hand, a bowl of golden fire—
while sounds the regimental choir!
Scarlet pelisses, warmly gleaming,
soon may you once more charm my eyes
in those grey minutes when sunrise
on the Hussars drawn up, half-dreaming,
and on their bivouac's woodland site,
throws down a furtive glint of light!

XXX

Avdotya Nikolavna's nearest
neighbour, none other than Garin,
twirling a whisker, with the clearest
of stares, sat there and drank her in.
He sensed how hard her heart was beating . . .
and suddenly he brushed, while eating—
I don't know how such things occur—
her foot, or slipper, with a spur.
This led to words of expiation,
and so a dialogue began;
two compliments, a tender scan—
and they were into explanation . . .
He was a gentleman—but she,
not quite the paragon she should be.

XXXI

She, though his tender words provided
a bliss she hastened to conceal,
by way of counterblast decided
on harmless friendship's dread ordeal—
a country-special, such rehearsal—
though torture's feminine-universal!
Yes, how all too familiar
friends' love, and ladies' friendship are!
And what infernal torture-sessions
some evening tête-à-têtes have seen
imposed by beauties of eighteen!*

XXXII

Last year I couldn't help observing,
in modish maidens round about,
ethereal manias, quite unnerving,
and mixed with mysticism. Look out!
For if your wife—that brilliant treasure—
at times of amatory leisure,
suddenly tries to make you see
that five is never two plus three,
or else, instead of flaming kisses,
she starts to magnetise you; oh,
go off to sleep—if you can go! . . .
The fruit of such analyses
the world of course has never known—
but I serve pragmatism alone.

* Three lines missing.

XXXIII

A splendid dance—but I won't answer
for a description of the ball.
It was an evening when my Lancer
found Cupid at his beck and call.
Alas! . . . now faith in Cupid falters,
and now we pray at other altars:
love's magic tsar's forgot and old;
long since, his sanctuary's gone cold!
But Petersburg's enlightenment
leaves the provincial far behind.*

XXXIV

Dunya by now had quite submitted;
his gaze had chained that heart of hers . . .
At home, through all her dreaming flitted
visions of sabres and of spurs.
She rose at nine o'clock next morning
and sat down in her nightdress, yawning,
at her embroidery's endless stream—
but it went on, that waking dream.
Her spouse was out—the jealous-yellow;
she was alone; her thoughts could dare!
A knock came at the door. "Who's there?
Andrew, Andrew, you lazy fellow! . . ."
She heard footsteps outside—but who
came in . . . was plainly no Andrew.

---

* Four lines missing.

XXXV

You'll have no trouble in surmising
who this unlooked-for guest could be.
Her suitor was too enterprising;
he went too fast, perhaps; but he
had shown much patience while he waited;
his rashness should be tolerated;
on balance you'll quite comprehend
what risks youth takes for such an end.
In total stillness, but inclining
his head, he came to Dunya, turned
upon her face a glance that yearned,
a gaze all misted with repining;
twisting his long moustache, he sighed
and, to her silence, thus replied:

XXXVI

"I know my visit's not expected—
it's in your eyes too clearly seen;
in love, you've never yet suspected
how much each day, each hour can mean!
With heart's turmoil excruciating,
there's no control, no means of waiting.
I'm here, to hazard on the line
my all . . . I'm your slave . . . and you're mine!
Society with its vulgar rattle
holds nothing that I'm frightened at;
I scorn the worldlings and their chat—
or else I'll die in pistol-battle . . .
Don't tremble! All must be avowed . . .
I know I'm loved . . . but say it loud! . . ."

XXXVII

His gaze, in bogus-humble fashion,
was bent on her; now it went dim;
and now, stoked-up with swooning passion,
the fire came blazing out from him.
Pale, and in prey to deep confusion,
she stood before him ... His conclusion
was that within a minute he
would reach love's triumph ... But then she
all of a sudden felt the riot
of an unwilled, unwitting shame—
and, flushing up as red as flame,
pushed him away from her: "Be quiet!
Go. I refuse to hear you out!
Leave me at once—or must I shout?"

XXXVIII

He looked: this was no sham, no foolish
play-acting, absolutely not,
but typically female, mulish
caprice—the devil take the lot!
And now ... the ultimate subjection!
Garin, in piteous genuflection,
entreats ... when suddenly the door
opens, her husband takes the floor.
The beauty: "Ah!" Close to exploding
they looked each other in the eye;
but silently the storm passed by.
Garin went home. There, after loading
pistols with ball, this prototype
of calm sat down—and lit a pipe.

XXXIX

Within the hour a servant hands him
a grubby note. The strangest twist!
The Treasurer himself demands him
that evening, for a game of whist:
it's his name-day—guests are invited ...
Enraged, astonished, and excited,
our hero was about to choke.
Was it some trick, some vicious joke?
He spent all day in cogitation.
Evening at last; he shot a look
out of the window: cunning crook!
House full; and what illumination!
But it may be as well to place
pistol in pocket—just in case?

XL

He goes in. She herself receives him,
with lowered gaze; and heaves a sigh
of such tremendous depth, it leaves him
speechless before he can reply.
About the morning's scene—no mention.
Once more they're strangers, at attention.
He talks about the weather; she
says "yes" or "no" or else "I see."
Distraught by anger and by worry,
into the study he'll proceed ...
For us to follow, there's no need—
and anyway it's wrong to hurry.
And so let's take a breather now—
we'll polish off this thing somehow.

XLI

I used to hurry once, pursuing
sensation, and the thrills it brought;
nature's wise laws, to my undoing,
mistakenly I set at nought.
With what result? Regret, and laughter!
Exhaustion chained my soul thereafter,
and, day and night, remorse went on
for times gone by. But what has gone
is past returning altogether.
So an imprisoned eaglet looks
round at the mountains and the brooks,
but never vainly preens a feather,
and never tears his bloodstained bait;
he's silent, and for death he'll wait.

XLII

Is that sweet age with us no longer
when things speak only to the heart,
when the heartbeat grows ever stronger,
and sparkling bliss is just a part
of life? Is thankless pain enraging
the eagle in his iron cageing?
No, no, his previous airborne way,
he'll rediscover it one day,
in lands where snow and mist are coating
the gloomy crag, the scowling crest,
where only eagles build their nest,
where caravans of cloud are floating—
there in luxurious rapture he
will spread his pinions, and be free!

XLIII

But everything must have an ending,
even most highfalutin dreams.
So back to work. Garin is wending
his way across the study. It seems
too strange! His host meets him, delighted,
seats him, and offers jam; excited,
he serves champagne. And as he drinks,
"You Judas!" so my Lancer thinks.
Tight-packed, a crowd of guests is dinning
round the green baize, to watch the game;
the play's been high; always the same,
the bank's been lucky, it's still winning.
The host himself has kept the bank
to oblige his comrades, while they drank.

XLIV

And so, while Treasurer Bobkovsky
is weightily employed quite near,
let me present the élite Tambovsky
society assembled here.
First comes the Counsellor, a battler
for virtue, and a non-stop prattler;
conscience and law by him are sold
with all alacrity, for gold;
the District President, he's lurking
inside his tie— tails on the floor,
whiskered, dull-eyed, a squeaking bore;
tirelessly for good order working,
here's the Inspector ... long ago
I've put his character on show.

XLV

Here, in short jacket, aromatic,
the Mitrofan* of the new wave,
illiterate, unsystematic,
already a consummate knave:
holding the Treasurer's application
and skill in highest estimation
he punts just as he's ordered to,
and feels quite honoured so to do.
There, too . . . but that will be sufficient
for you, dear reader; all this stuff
is anyway diffuse enough
without the extra coefficient
added when pens begin to think,
and by the waywardness of ink.

XLVI

The game went on. This player, ashen,
tore up the cards, and screamed; the cost
appalled that one—in idiot-fashion
he dared not credit what he'd lost.
Meanwhile the play had favoured others
who, drinking noisily, like brothers
clinked glasses. Silent gloom beset
the banker now. An icy sweat
along his shiny scalp was oozing.
He heard once more the run of play
which took his whole estate away.
Finally, quite unhinged by losing,
he staked his mansion, lose or win,
with all its chattels, out or in.

* Spoilt, ignorant young boor in Fonvizin's play *Nedorosl* (*The Minor*).

XLVII

He lost. His drozhky went, his carriage,
three horses, with two yokes he'd got,
earrings the partner of his marriage
had on, his chairs—the whole damned lot.
As white as death, with eyeballs staring,
he sat there silent and despairing.
Already a sputtering candle went
out, and the night was nearly spent.
A blueish-whiteish gleam of morning
along the clouded heavens crept.
The fact that none of them had slept
on all the gamblers was just dawning—
when suddenly the Treasurer woke,
called for attention, and then spoke.

XLVIII

With dignity he asked permission
for one more hand; in a nutshell:
to win back all—on one condition:
"if not, I lose my wife as well."
Oh shock! oh horror without measure!
How ever could they at the Treasure
have stood the man! In the turmoil
the guests felt scorched with burning oil.
Alone, with an ice-cold reaction,
Garin goes up to him. "I'm glad,"
he says: "just let them shout like mad;
we'll solve this to our satisfaction,
only remember, please: no tricks—
or else you'll find you're in a fix!"

XLIX

Now I present for your inspection
the ring of gamblers round about,
the different hues of their complexion,
as eyes and spectacles flash out.
Our whiskered hero does his punting
from where he stands erect, confronting,
between two candles, an immense
cranium, that wears a not-so-dense
mesh of grey curls diffusely dotted,
a mouth distorted in a grin,
hands on the pack—there, I've filled in
the whole tableau; of course you've spotted
the Treasurer's wife, who's in a chair
in that far corner over there.

L

What pangs, what passions, what affliction
she suffered, I can't start to explain;
but from her face it's my conviction,
if you could have divined her pain,
or guessed the secret in her keeping,
you would perforce have burst out weeping.
But let no sympathetic tear
darken your eye. Absurd, I fear,
is pity or commiseration
in one who's lived, and knows the world!
Invented sorrows, once unfurled
in a more feeling generation,
quite often prompted tears ... but I
ask you ... who profited thereby?

LI

The battle was quite soon concluded;
wildly the Lancer played, and luck
mocked the old man, as one deluded—
the die was cast . . . the hour had struck . . .
Avdotya, long since agonising,
in silence from her armchair rising,
swimmingly to the table walked—
her countenance was all that talked:
it was ash-pale. The assembly started
in blank amazement. All await
rebukes, complaints, or tears . . . But straight
upon the Treasurer she darted
a glance, and then went on to fling
into his face her wedding-ring—

LII

and fainted. Snatching up the beauty,
forgetting sabre, cap, and sense,
the Lancer with his precious booty
set off for home . . . Next day, intense
gossip, some laughable, some witty,
convulsed the honourable city—
for a whole week; of those who spoke,
some thought it serious, some a joke.
All talked of it, the theme was burning.
The old man found defenders, and,
by ladies, Garin out of hand
was damned—what for?—no way of learning.
Envy, perhaps? but no, no, no!
I do despise all slander so.

LIII

Thus my sad anecdote's unfolded,
my fable, to be more exact.
Admit it now, I'm to be scolded?
You had expected passion-packed
drama? Now everyone wants passion;
even for ladies, blood's in fashion . . .
Just like a schoolboy calling *pax*,
I've stopped my tale at its climax.
With simple swooning it's immoral,
it's tasteless to conclude a scene;
no reconcilement has there been,
not even any proper quarrel . . .
What happened? Friends, my story's through;
it's gone quite far enough for you.

THE NOVICE*

I did but taste a little honey, and, lo, I must die.

1 SAMUEL XIV:43

I

Once, not so many years ago,
where soundingly together flow
Arágva and Kurá—the place
where, like two sisters, they embrace—
there stood a monastery. Still
the traveller who comes down the hill
sees pillars of a crumbling gate,
towers, a church's vaulted state;
but from it now there's no perfume
of incense smoking in the gloom;
and late at night no chanting rolls,
no monks are praying for our souls.
Just an old watchman, feeble, grey,
attends the ruined church today;
by men forgotten he has been,
also by death, as he sweeps clean
gravestones with legends which keep green
tales of past fame—of how, worn down
beneath the burden of his crown,
a certain king conveyed his land,
in such a year, to Russia's hand.

* Lermontov's title for the poem is *Mtsyri*. He explains in a note: "*Mtsyri* in the Georgian language means 'a monk who does not serve,' something in the nature of a 'novice.'"

And so heaven's benediction fell
on Georgia!—it has blossomed well;
the hedge that friendly bayonets made
since then has kept it unafraid,
enclosed in its own garden-shade.

II

Down from the mountains rode one day
a Russian general, on his way
to Tiflis, with a prisoner-child—
the boy was ill, the road had piled
up too much effort for him: wild
as mountain chamois, about six,
pliant and weak as kindling-sticks.
But in him his exhausted plight
had called forth some ancestral might
of spirit. For however faint
he felt, no groan, no least complaint
passed those young lips; he thrust aside
all ordinary food; in pride
and in silence he all but died.
A monk took pity on the waif,
tended his malady, and safe
in sheltering walls he lived on there,
brought back to health by loving care.
At first, detesting childish fun,
he ran away from everyone,
and, roaming silent, all alone,
looked to the east with sigh and groan—
yearnings too deep to understand
turned him towards his native land.
But soon his prison sentence grew
familiar, the strange language too;

then, christened by that holy man,
he never knew the world; his plan
in the full prime of youth was now
to utter the monastic vow;
when suddenly, one autumn night,
he vanished—disappeared from sight.
Hills darkly wooded rose all round.
For three long days they searched the ground,
in vain; then on the steppe they found
him fainted, once more brought him in
back to the cloister; he was thin
and deathly pale and feeble too,
as from some fever he'd been through,
some hunger, while he'd been away,
or some ordeal. No word he'd say
to questions, visibly each day
he faded and approached his end.
Then came to him his reverend friend
with exhortation and with prayer;
proudly the sufferer heard him there,
then raised himself with all the strength
still left him, and thus spoke at length:

III

"I thank you, sir, for coming here
for my confession. In your ear
words are the medicine that best
will ease the burden of my chest.
To others I have done no ill,
and so my actions for you will
be profitless to hear about—
or can a soul be detailed out?
I've lived my short life in duress.

No, two such lives—for one of stress
and terror, willingly I would
exchange them if I only could.
I've known one thought, one and the same,
a thought of passion and of flame:
worm-like, it lived in me; it ate
my soul away like fire in grate.
My dreams, from stifling cell's estate,
my prayers, it called to that brave world
where fears and battles are unfurled,
where lost in cloud are cliff and scree,
and where, like eagles, men are free.
This passion, in the dark midnight
nourished on tears, with all my might
to heaven and earth I shout today,
and for no pardon do I pray.

IV

"Often I've heard how you did save
me, sir, from an untimely grave—
for what? . . . alone, and glum, and pale,
a leaf torn off by blast of gale,
I've grown up within walls of gloom,
in soul a child, a monk by doom.
'Mother' and 'father'—holy sounds—
I could call no one; in the bounds
of sanctuary you hoped I'd lose
the natural human wish to use
these sweetest of all names. In vain:
they were inborn. Once and again
others I saw on every hand
with home, friends, parents, native land;
for me, not only no one dear—

not even dear ones' tombs were here!
Then, without wasting time to weep,
I took an oath I swore to keep:
that at some time my burning breast
just for a moment should be pressed
against someone's, perhaps unknown,
yet from a land that was my own.
But now, alas, they're dead, those dreams
in the full beauty of their gleams,
and, as I've lived, I'll find my grave
in alien soil, an orphaned slave.

V

"I have no horror of the tomb:
they say that suffering, in that room,
sleeps in cold, everlasting calm.
But, to stop living, . . . there's the harm.
I'm young, young . . . Have you never known
the dreams to which wild youth is prone?
Have you not known, have you forgot,
how hate was sharp, how love was hot;
how the heart beat more keenly while
from some tall battlemented pile
you saw the sun, the fields spread round,
and air was nipping, and you found
deep in the wall's recess sometimes
a huddled nursling from far climes—
a young dove that, driven in by fear
of raging storms, has fluttered here?
Perhaps the glorious world today
has cooled for you: you're weak, you're grey,
you've lost the habit of desire.
But you no longer need that fire.

You've got things to forget—for you,
you've lived—I wish I could live too!

VI

"You ask what I contrived to see
during the days while I was free?
Rich plains, and hills that trees had crowned,
woods running riot all around,
in whispering clusters, fresh as spring,
like brothers dancing in a ring.
And frowning cliffs I saw, whose heart
cleft by the torrent, beat apart;
I guessed their thoughts: diviner's art
was given to me from on high!
their stone embracings in the sky
long since cut off, each day, each night,
they long, they thirst to reunite;
but years and ages pass in vain—
and never they shall join again!
And I saw mountain crests that seem
fantastical as any dream,
where, at the earliest hour of dawn,
as if from altars, smoke was drawn
up from the peaks into the blue,
and little clouds came swarming through,
leaving their secret sleeping-place,
turning to east their hurrying face—
in a white caravan, like bands
of birds flown in from distant lands!
Far off I saw, through vapoury strands,
where, glittering diamond of the snows,
grey bastion-Caucasus arose;
and then, for some strange reason, I

felt light of heart; in days gone by—
a secret voice so prompted me—
I'd lived there. I began to see
ever more clearly, now at last,
places and things from time long past.

VII

"And I remembered father's hall,
and our ravine, our village, all
in cool shadow dispersed around;
I heard the evening thunder-sound
as homing horses galloped through,
the distant bark of dogs I knew.
On moonlight evenings, memory traced
the row of elders, swarthy-faced,
who sat with serious looks before
my father's porch; no, I saw more,
I saw the chiselled scabbards gleam,
on their long daggers ... Like a dream
a row of pictures, indistinct,
came and before my vision winked.
My father, as in life, all prinked
in armour, stood there; chain-mail clinked
as I remembered; light ablaze
from rifle-barrels, and that gaze,
that proud, indomitable stare;
and my young sisters too were there ...
their sweet eyes shone, their voices rang,
once more I listened as they sang
over my crib ... A torrent sprang
down our ravine; it roared, it rolled,
but it was shallow; on its gold
sands I would play at noon; my sight

pursued the swallows in their flight
as, when a storm of rain was due,
they grazed the water while they flew.
I saw again our peaceful hall;
at evening, round the hearth, we all
listened to tales that would recall
how men lived in days long since gone,
days when the world still brighter shone.

VIII

"What did I do, you seek to know,
while I had freedom? I *lived*—so
my life were sadder far than this
dotage of yours, had it to miss
those three days of perfected bliss.
It's long since I began to yearn
to see far fields, and to discern
if earth was beautiful—to learn
whether for freedom or for gaol
we come to this terrestrial vale.
So in that dreadful hour of night
when thunder struck you down with fright,
when by the altar, pressing round,
you lay all prostrate on the ground,
I fled. I'd have been glad to race,
to enfold in brotherly embrace
that storm! My gaze pursued each cloud,
my hands caught lightning-bolts ... Speak loud,
tell me, inside this walled-in space
what would you give me to replace
the friendship, keen, though brief and frail,
that stormy hearts feel for the gale?

IX

"And so I ran, long hours and far,
I know not where! No single star
lighted me on my stumbling way.
Joyful it was for me to stray,
to let my tortured chest assay
the midnight freshness of the wood—
no more than that. I ran a good
long while, and then, worn out at last,
lay on a tussock thickly grassed,
and listened: no sounds of a chase.
The storm had died. A feeble trace
of light, a radiance, seemed to lie
between the earth and the dark sky,
and, patterned on it, stood out plain
the peaks of a far mountain-chain.
Silent, unmoving and unseen,
I lay; at times, from the ravine,
like a small child, a jackal wailed,
and smoothly, glitteringly scaled,
between the stones a serpent slipped;
and yet my soul was never gripped
by fear: wild as a beast, I slid,
snakelike, away from man, and hid.

X

"Storm-swollen, on the lower ground
a torrent roared, and its dull sound
resembled closely, so I found,
a hundred angry voices. I
could understand this wordless cry,
this unformed murmur—endless shock

of wrangling with hard-fronted rock.
Now all at once the tumult fell
silent, now it began to swell
and break the stillness all about;
soon, on that misty height, rang out
the song of birds, and then the east
turned golden; suddenly released,
a breath shook leaves on every bough;
the sleepy flowers breathed perfume now,
and, like them, I saluted day,
looked out . . . and it's no shame to say,
as I peered round, I quaked with fear:
I had been lying on the sheer
brink of a frightful cliff; from here
an angry torrent, far below,
went whirling onward, and to show
the way down, steps cut in the face;
only a fiend expelled from grace,
thrown down from heaven, could ever dare
to seek hell's caverns down that stair.

XI

"And, all around, God's garden bloomed.
Flowers that in bright raiment loomed
still kept a trace of tears divine,
and curling tendrils of the vine
wound brilliantly amid the sheen
cast by the leaves' pellucid green;
while, on them, heavy clusters slung
were like rich earrings as they hung
in splendour; sometimes to them flew
a flock of birds in timorous crew.
Once more I lay back on the ground,

once more I listened to that sound,
to those strange voices in the scrub
whispering away to every shrub
as if they had, by magic spell,
secrets of earth and sky to tell;
all nature's voices there were blurred
together; nowhere to be heard
one single human tongue to raise
the morning hour's majestic praise.
All that I felt then, all my mind
was thinking, left no trace behind;
if only I could tell it—then
just for a flash I'd live again.
Heaven's vault, it was so clear and chaste
that morning, sharp eyes could have traced
the flight of angels; through and through,
such even, deep, translucent blue!
My eyes and my soul drowned; but soon
under the blaze of sultry noon
my reveries were all dispersed
and I began to pine with thirst.

XII

"Then to the torrent from that height,
from crag to crag, as best I might,
clutching the pliant bushes, I
set off downhill. A rock would fly
from underfoot, and roll and bound;
smoking, the dust behind it wound;
it rumbled down, with jump and thud,
and then was swallowed in the flood;
dangling, I hung above the scree,
but death held no alarms for me,

for hands are strong when youth is free!
As I groped down the steep descent,
the mountain water's freshness went
aloft to meet me, and I fell
thirstily on the torrent-swell.
Then, all at once, a voice—and light
footfalls . . . and in instinctive fright
I ducked behind the scrub, and out
timidly I peered round about,
I listened with a kind of thirst.
And ever nearer, burst by burst,
the Georgian maiden's singing rang;
with such an artlessness she sang,
so sweet and clear and free her tone,
you'd think she'd learnt to sing alone
the names of loved ones of her own.
Nothing more simple than that strain,
but in my thought it lodged; again
at nightfall I can hear it ring,
as if, unseen, her soul should sing.

XIII

"Holding her pitcher on her head,
the maiden took the path that led
down to the mountain torrent's bed.
Sometimes, on rock, her foothold slipped;
she laughed as awkwardly she tripped.
Her dress was humble; down the track
she walked lightfooted and brushed back
her winding *chadra*. Sultry days
had covered in a golden haze
her face, her breast; and summer's glow
breathed from her mouth and cheeks. But so

deep was the darkness of her eyes,
so full of secrets to surmise,
love-secrets, that my head went round.
All I remember is the sound
the jug made as it slowly drowned,
a murmuring through the torrent flood ...
When I came to, and when the blood
had flowed back from my heart, she'd gone
some distance off; as she walked on,
slow, yet lightfooted, straight and trim
beneath her load, she was as slim
as any poplar-tree that stands
and queens it over neighbouring lands!
Not far away, in close embrace,
two cabins grown from the rock-face
loomed through the chilly evening mist;
above one's roof, in a blue twist,
smoke rose. As now, I see again
how the door gently opened, then
it shut once more! ... For you, I know,
it's past conceiving why I'm so
brimful of yearning and so sad—
it's past conceiving, and I'm glad;
the memory of those moments I
would wish in me, with me to die.

XIV

"By the night's travail quite worn out
I lay down in the shades. Without
effort my eyes were sealed about
by blissful sleep ... I saw once more
that Georgian girl and, as before,
a strange, sweet yearning came to break

my heart and make it pine and ache.
I fought, I fought to breathe—but soon
I woke up. And by now the moon
was high and shining; after it
a single cloudlet seemed to flit
with arms wide open for the embrace.
And the dark world was still; in space
far distant, ranges tipped with snow
sparkled away, and seemed to throw
a silhouette of silvery glow.
Splashing its banks, I heard the stream;
and in the cabin a faint gleam
would flicker up, and once more die;
just so, across the midnight sky,
a bright star shines, then dies up there!
I longed to ... but I didn't dare
go over to the hut. I'd planned
one thing—to reach my native land;
one thing alone—so hunger's pain
I quelled as best I could. Again
I started on the straightest way,
timid, without a word to say—
but all at once began to stray
as soon as in the forest's night
I'd lost the mountains from my sight.

XV

"In my despair, to no avail,
I clutched, at moments on my trail,
some thorny bush, with ivy crowned:
eternal forest all around
grew denser, grimmer, every pace;
with million coal-black eyes, the face

of darkest night looked through the scrub,
peered through the twigs of every shrub . . .
My head was turning; for a time
I tried the trees, began to climb;
but always, on the horizon's edge,
the same woods rose in spire and wedge.
Then I threw myself down and lay
sobbing in a despairing way,
biting the earth's damp breast; a spell
of weeping came, and my tears fell
to ground in scalding streams of dew . . .
but help from men, I swear to you,
I'd have at no price . . . Through and through,
like a steppe beast, to all their crew
I felt a stranger; and if my
weak tongue had by the feeblest cry
betrayed me, reverend father, why,
I'd torn it out, as I may die.

XVI

"You will recall, no teardrop came
from me in childhood; all the same
I now was weeping without shame.
For who could see except the dark
forest, the moon high on its arc?
Lit by its rays, all floored with sand
and moss, I saw before me stand,
impenetrably walled, a glade.
Suddenly there, a flickering shade,
two sparks of fire that darted round . . .
from the dark forest in one bound
a creature sprang, rolled on its back,
lay playing on the sandy track.

It was the waste's eternal guest—
the huge snow-leopard. He caressed
a moistened bone, he gnawed it, squealed
for sheer enjoyment; then he wheeled
on the full moon his bloodshot eyes,
thumping his tail in friendliest wise—
his coat with silver gleams was shot.
I waited for the fight; I'd got
in hand a cudgel—and on fire
my heart with sudden wild desire
for war and blood . . . yes, fate, I'll say,
has led me on a different way . . .
but if I'd lived at home, I swear
I'd never have been counted there
as one of those who feared to dare.

XVII

"I waited. Now, through shades of dark,
he smelt an enemy—and hark,
a sad howl, like a groan, drawn out,
came forth . . . In rage he set about
to paw and furrow up the sand,
he reared right up, as people stand,
he crouched, and his first furious leap
threatened me with eternal sleep.
But I forestalled him, and my stroke
was sure and swift. My cudgel broke
open his wide brow like an axe . . .
He toppled over in his tracks,
groaned like a man. But now once more,
though blood was streaming from his score
in a broad, thickly pulsing vein,
the mortal fight boiled up again.

XVIII

"He rushed my chest in one swift bound;
but with my weapon I had found
his throat, twice I had turned it round . . .
he whined, and with his final strength
began to jerk and twitch; at length,
like a snake-couple tight-enlaced,
more closely than two friends embraced,
we fell together, in dark night
continued on the ground our fight.
And at that moment I was wild
and fiercer than the desert's child,
the snow-leopard; like him, I blazed,
I howled—as if I had been raised
by leopards and by wolves beneath
the woods' cool overhanging sheath.
It seemed as if I'd lost the power
of human language—in that hour
my chest brought out a wild sound—why,
it seemed from childhood never I
had learned to make a different cry . . .
But weakness now crept on my foe,
he tossed, he turned, he breathed more slow,
he crushed me one last time . . . in ire
his staring pupils threatened fire—
then gently closed up in the deep
onset of everlasting sleep;
but, meeting death, he knew to keep
facing it and his conquering foe,
the way a fighting man should go!

XIX

"You see these deep scars on my chest
scooped where the leopard-talons pressed;
they haven't grown together, still
they gape; but earth's damp cover will
bring them the freshness of the field,
by death for ever they'll be healed.
I forgot all about them then,
called my reserves of strength again,
in deepest forest plunged in straight . . .
But all in vain my fight with fate:
it laughed at me and my estate!

XX

"I left the woodland. Now the day
was waking up; before its ray
the dance of travelling stars went out.
Then the dark forest all about
began to talk. From an *aül**
far off, smoke started up. A full
boom from the gorge, a voiceless hum
blew on the wind . . . I heard it come,
I sat and listened; but it died
just as the breeze did. Far and wide
I turned my gaze: that countryside,
surely I knew it? And a strong
terror came over me, for long
I couldn't credit that once more
I'd headed back to prison; or
that all these days I'd spent in vain
nursing my secret hope—the pain,

* Moslem village.

the yearning patience every hour,
and all for what?... That in the flower
of years, and hardly having seen
God's world, that having scarcely been
allowed in murmuring woods to know
the bliss of freedom, I must go
and carry with me to the tomb
the longing for my home, the gloom
of cheated hope and of self-blame,
of your compassion and its shame!...
Still sunk in doubt, I lingered there,
I thought it all was some nightmare ...
Suddenly in the silence fell
once more the distant tolling bell
and all was lucid in no time ...
At once I'd recognised its chime!
How often from my childish eyes
it had chased out the bright disguise
of dreamland, forms of kith and kin,
the steppe's wild liberty, the spin
of lightfoot horses, and the shocks
of splendid fights among the rocks,
and I the winner!... So I heard,
tearless and strengthless. In a word
it seemed my heart was where the chime
came from—as if someone each time
struck it with iron. Then I knew,
though vaguely, nothing I could do
would to my homeland bring me through.

XXI

"Yes, I've deserved my destined course!
On the strange steppe a mighty horse,
with its unskilful rider thrown,

from far off will find out alone
the straightest, shortest homeward way . . .
I cannot equal him. Each day
in vain my heart desires and yearns;
feeble the flame with which it burns,
plaything of dreams, malaise of mind.
On me my prison left behind
its brand . . . Just so there grows in gaol
on the wet flags, alone and pale,
a blossom, and long time puts out
no youthful leaves, but waits about,
languishing for life-giving rays.
It waits, and there pass many days
till some kind hand, touched by the grief
of the poor bloom, to bring relief
moves it to a rose-garden, where
from every side there breathes an air
of life and sweetness . . . But, once there,
no sooner comes the sunrise hour
than with its incandescent power
it scorches the gaol-nurtured flower.

XXII

"Just like that blossom, I was burned
by day's remorseless fire. I turned
to no avail my weary head,
I hid it in the grass; instead
my brow by withered leaf was wreathed
in thorny crown, and the earth breathed
into my face its breath of flame.
High up above me circling came
motes in the sun; the vapour steamed
from the white rocks. God's whole world seemed
numbed in a heavy slumber there,

the deep dull slumber of despair.
If only a corncrake from the hill
had called; if only the quick trill
of dragonfly wings, or a rill
childishly chattering ... Just a snake
was rustling through the dried-up brake;
across its yellow back, light played
as if upon a golden blade
engraved all down with letters, and
scattering a small wake of sand
it crawled meticulously, then
it played, it basked, it writhed again
in triple coil, then gave a start,
just as if scalded, in one dart
it dived inside the bushes' heart,
and deep in scrub it disappeared.

XXIII

"But now the sky was calm, and cleared
of cloudscape. Far, through mists that steamed,
rose two dark mountains, and there gleamed
underneath one of them a wall—
our cloister's battlemented hall.
Arágva and Kurá below
were lapping with their silvery flow
at feet of islands cool and fresh,
at whispering bushes and their mesh
of roots, and pulsing on their way
in gentle harmony ... but they
were too far off! I tried to rise—
everything whirled before my eyes;
I tried to shout—my dried-up tongue,
voiceless and motionless it hung ...

I seemed to die. Herald of death,
a madness crushed me, squeezed my breath.
And then it seemed to me that I
on the moist bed had come to lie
of a deep river—there I found
mysterious darkness all around.
And quenching my eternal thirst
the ice-cold stream, in bubbling burst,
into my chest came flowing deep . . .
My only fear, to fall asleep,
so sweet, so blissful was my plight . . .
And there above me in the height
wave thronged on wave, and through the bright
crystal of water the sun beamed,
with a moon's graciousness it gleamed . . .
From time to time, across its ray
fish in bright flocks began to play.
And one, more friendly than her mates,
caressed me. Backed with scaly plates
of gold, I still can see her coat,
as round my head she came to float;
and, deeply gazing, her green eyes
were sweetly sad . . . and a profound
amazement seized me at the sound
of her small voice's silvery strain:
it sang to me, then ceased again.

That voice, it seemed to say: 'My child,
    do thou stay here with me:
our life down in this watery wild
    is cool, and rich, and free.

'My sisters all I will enrol
    and with our circling dance

we shall divert thy weary soul
　　and cheer thy fainting glance.

'Now sleep away, soft is thy bed,
　　thy sheet, shot through with gleams.
The years, the ages o'er thy head
　　will pass in wondrous dreams.

'Beloved, let me tell thee true,
　　I love thee, as down here
the current flowing freely through
　　and my own life are dear ...'

Long, long I listened; and I found
the stream had set its quiet sound,
the tale its lilting whisper told,
to music from that fish of gold.
I swooned. The light that God had lit
quenched in my eyes. The raving fit
passed from my fainting body then.

XXIV

"So I was found, brought here again ...
I've finished, for you know what more
there is to tell. Believe me or
believe me not—I do not care.
Just one thing grieves me, this I swear:
my body, lifeless, cold and dumb,
will never to my homeland come
to moulder there; my grievous thrall
in the deaf circle of this wall
will never be rehearsed, or claim
a sad repute for my dim name.

XXV

"Father, your hand, please, in farewell;
mine is on fire, as you can tell . . .
Since childhood, well-concealed, suppressed,
this flame has lived inside my breast;
but now there's nothing left that burns;
it's blazed its way out, and returns,
returns once more to Him who gives
just measure, to each man who lives,
of pain and peace . . . but what do I
care? Yes, in realms behind the sky
my soul will find its refuge due . . .
alas! I'd barter, for a few
moments among those steep and strange
rocks where my childhood used to range—
heaven and eternity I'd change . . .

XXVI

"But when I'm dying—for that date,
believe me, there's not long to wait—
give orders I be carried out
into our garden, just about
where bloom two white acacias, where
the turf's so thick, and the cool air
so perfumed, and the leaves that play
so limpid-gold in the sun's ray!
There bid them set me; of bright day
and the sky's radiant blue I will
there for the last time drink my fill.
Thence Caucasus is clear to see!
perhaps, down from his summit, he
will send me, on the wind's cool breath,

his farewell ... and before my death
perhaps near by once more I'll hear
my native tongue! and someone dear,
I'll dream, some brother, or some friend,
how, gently, over me he'll bend,
how, tenderly, he'll wipe my brow
clean of death's icy sweat, and how
he'll sing to me in undertone
of that dear country, once my own ...
and so I'll sleep—no curse, no groan!"

THE DEMON

An Eastern Story

PART I

I

A Demon, soul of all the banished,
sadly above the sinful world
floated, and thoughts of days now vanished
before him crowdingly unfurled;
days when, in glory's habitation,
he shone out a pure cherubim,
when comets flying on their station
rejoiced to exchange a salutation
of welcome and of love with him,
when through the vapours of creation,
hungry for knowledge, he flew on
with caravans in their migration
to space where headlong stars have gone;
with love and faith to lean upon,
happy first-born of our condition,
he knew no evil, no suspicion,
his mind undaunted by the length
of fruitless aeons sadly falling . . .
so much, so much there was . . . the strength,
the will now fails him for recalling!

II

He wandered, now long-since outcast;
his desert had no refuge in it:
and one by one the ages passed,

as minute follows after minute,
each one monotonously dull.
The world he ruled was void and null;
the ill he sowed in his existence
brought no delight. His technique scored,
he found no traces of resistance—
yet evil left him deeply bored.

III

Above the steep Caucasian places
heaven's expatriate flew full-pelt:
below him, Kazbek's diamond-faces
glittered with snows that never melt,
and far beneath them, dark, arresting
as some crevasse where snakes are nesting,
Daryal wound its twisted belt,
and Terek, lioness-like, was springing,
shaggily-maned all down its back;
it roared, and mountain beasts and swinging
birds high on their circuitous track
in the azure heard its lilting water;
and clouds from far-off southern lands
escorted him in gilded bands
toward horizon's northern quarter;
and closely packed massifs of stone,
deep-sunk in their mysterious dreaming
had bowed their peaks as he had flown
above the bed where waves were gleaming;
and towered castles on the hard
precipice-top, above the entry
to Caucasus, in cloud stood guard
grim as some Cyclopean sentry!
How strange, how savage was the whole

divine landscape; but that proud soul
viewed with disdain and some derision
the product of his Maker's will;
his lofty forehead at this vision
expressed no thought, exactly nil.

IV

Before him now the picture changes;
a different scene, a brilliant hue:
luxurious Georgia's vales and ranges
are counterpaned-out for his view;
fortunate land, and sumptuous too!
Pillar-like ruined halls and granges,
and watercourses that run loud,
over the dappled pebbles rolling,
and nightingales that in the crowd
of roses voice their amorous trolling
to which no answer is allowed;
plane-trees inside their ivy sheathing
with branching shadows; caves where deer
at flaming midday hide their fear;
and life, and sound of leaves, and glow,
a hundred tongues that murmur low,
and plants in thousands gently breathing!
The sensual heat of high noondays,
nights which the never-failing sprays
of dew have drenched in aromatic,
and stars like eyes, clear and dramatic,
sharp as a Georgian maiden's gaze! . . .
and yet, apart from envy's chilling,
this natural glory could inspire
the barren exile with no thrilling
of new emotion or new fire;

and everything he contemplated
he either scorned or execrated.

V

A lofty hall, a broad courtyard,
grey-haired Gudál built for his pleasure . . .
the building cost his slaves much treasure
of tears and labour long and hard.
His towers in light of morning barred
with stripes of shade the mountain fairway.
Out of the cliff was hacked a stairway
from where the angled bastions gleam
down to the river; Gudál's daughter,
white-veiled and flashing like a dream,
Princess Tamara, seeking water
runs down to the Arágva's stream.

VI

From the steep mountain every minute
the voiceless house stares at the vale;
today, though, there's a feast, pipes wail—
the hall resounds, wine's flowing in it,
for Gudál has betrothed his girl,
the whole clan's here, all's in a whirl.
Up on the roof, among her bidden
girl-friends, the bride looks on the hall:
sitting on rugs, they sing and call
and play. Already sunk and hidden
by distant peaks the sun's half-ball;
to keep the measure of their singing
the girls clap hands; the youthful bride

takes up her tambourine and, swinging
it round her head in sweeping-wide
circles, abruptly starts to glide;
one moment, like a bird, she dashes
and swoops; the next, she stands at gaze
and her moist eyes dart out their rays
from underneath malicious lashes;
and now she twitches a dark brow,
now suddenly she stops her gliding,
and halts, and makes a little bow;
meanwhile a heavenly foot is sliding
over the carpet; infantile
is the enjoyment in her smile.
Even the moonbeam's fitful shivers
playing on water can't in truth
rival that peerless smile: it quivers
as full of joy as life, or youth.

VII

I swear it on the midnight star,
on rays of sunset or of dawning,
never did autocrat of far
golden Iran, or earthly tsar,
kiss such an eye; on sultry morning
no sparkling fount of the harēm
ever in summertime was splashing
a waist so heavenly in the flashing,
the pearly dewfall of its stream!

Or by no human fingers, pressing
a loved one's brow in their caressing,
was ever hair like this undone;

since earth lost heaven, with humble duty
I swear it, never did such beauty
blossom beneath the southern sun.

VIII

She'd dance no more. Alas, there waited
a different morrow; she was fated,
she, heiress of the celebrated
Gudál, she, lively freedom's own
nursling, to grim incarceration,
vowed to a strange expatriation
and to a family unknown.
Sometimes a secret hesitation
obscured the brilliance of her face;
and, with her, every single motion
was so compact of inner notion,
full of such sweet and simple grace,
that if the Demon, as he floated
above, had looked upon the bride,
thinking of brothers once devoted
he would have turned away—and sighed . . .

IX

And he did see her . . . For a second
by turmoil too deep to be reckoned
the Demon sensed that he was bound.
His dumb soul's emptiness was slowly
filled with loud chords of blissful sound—
and once again he reached that holy
shrine where love, beauty, goodness gleam! . . .
And long he gazed, with fascination,

at the sweet view; as if in dream
his earlier blisses' constellation
came as on summons from afar
and swam before him, star on star.
Then, riveted by unseen forces,
he came to feel a new sorrow;
emotion started on discourses
in language that he used to know.
Was this a sign of new begetting?
the cunning, covetousness-whetting
words came no more . . . had he forgot?
God never gave that: and *he'd* not
at any price accept forgetting . . .
. . . .

X

At sunset, spurring on his beast,
the bridegroom to the wedding feast
with all impatient haste was riding,
and the green banks of brightly gliding
Arágva he had safely gained.
Behind him staggered, limped and strained
an endless line of camels bringing
his wedding gifts in towering load;
they gleamed, and all their bells were ringing
as they strung out along the road.
Sinodal's lord himself was heading
the sumptuous caravan. His waist
inside its belt is tightly laced;
sabre and dagger-mounts are shedding
the sun's reflections; his flintlock,
slung back, has notches on its stock.
And in the wind his sleeves are straying,

sleeves of a *chukha** that all round
with trimming of galloon is crowned.

A saddle where bright silks are playing;
a bit with tassels downward swaying;
and, lathered under him, his bold
charger with that rare hue of gold.
Karabakh's brave offspring, ears with tension
pricked, all taut in apprehension
snorts as he squints down in the gloom
on the careering river's spume.
A path to make the bravest shiver!
The cliff to leftward; deep as doom,
to right the chasm of the wild river.
It's late; on snowy peaks the sliver
of radiance fades; mists rise apace . . .
the caravan begins to race.

XI

A wayside chapel . . . here is sleeping
since days of old, in God's good keeping,
now sanctified, an ancient prince
cut down by vengeance. Ever since,
heading for feast or bloody fighting,
here, as he hurried on his way,
the traveller never missed inditing
the strongest prayer that he could say:
that prayer, so fervently directed,
kept him from Moslem's knife protected.
But the bold bridegroom now disdained
the rite his forefathers maintained.

* Outer garment with sleeves that fold back. (*Lermontov's note.*)

The crafty Demon with infernal
reveries had tempted him; in thought
beneath the gloom, the shades nocturnal,
it was his sweetheart's lips he sought.
But suddenly, ahead, a figure—
no, two—no, more—a shot—whose trigger?
In clinking stirrups rising now,
ramming his fur cap on his brow
the dauntless prince in silence lifted
his Turkish whip; it flashed, it whirred,
crack went the lash; he spoke no word
as, eagle-like, he swooped, he shifted . . .
Another shot! a screaming man—
then from the valley dull groans rended
the still of night. The Georgians ran,
the battle all too soon was ended!

XII

Now calm returned; the sheepish flock
of camels on the road, in shock,
gazed back upon the dead, astounded;
and in the still of steppe and rock
dully their little bells resounded.
The sumptuous caravan was sacked;
above those Christian corpses packed
the bird of night invigilated!
no peaceful sepulchre awaited
their bodies, in some cloister's trust,
where rested their forefather's dust;
no sisters and no mothers, trailing
lengths of impenetrable veiling,
with sobs and prayers and sighs and wailing
visit their grave and mourn their loss!

And yet, by loving hands erected
here at the highway verge, protected
by the steep cliff, there stands a cross;
in spring the amorous, neglected
ivy, in emerald nets displayed,
clasps it in tenderest embraces;
and, turning in from far-off places,
the walker, tired from the long grade,
rests in the consecrated shade . . .

XIII

Swift as a deer the horse is rushing,
snorting as if for battle; hushing
sometimes, he halts in mid-career,
blows out his nostrils wide in fear,
and listens to the breeze's sighing;
now thunderously his hooves are flying,
beating tattoos of rhythmic sort;
his mane all tangled, wildly spraying,
he gallops on without a thought.
He bears a silent horseman, swaying
across the saddle or, down-pressed,
collapsed upon that golden crest.
His hand no longer steers the bridle,
feet in the stirrups are thrust back,
bloodstreams are flowing, broad and idle,
across the cloth of his shabrack.
Brave galloper, you brought your master
out from the battle like a dart,
but the Ossetian's bullet, faster
than you, in darkness found his heart!

XIV

In Gudál's hall there's grief and moaning,
the guests swarm out to the courtyard;
whose charger, broken past atoning,
outside the gates has fallen so hard?
and who's the lifeless rider? traces
of war's alarm lurk in the spaces
of his dark-favoured, furrowed brow.
On clothes, on weapons, blood is freezing;
his hand in a last furious squeezing
upon the mane is frozen now . . .
Oh, not for long the bride had waited
her young groom's coming: and at least,
his princely word unviolated,
he galloped to the wedding feast . . .
Alas, no more that brave, hard-bitten
charger shall bear him—so it's written! . . .

XV

Heaven's punishment like thunder swooped
down on that family, so light-hearted!
pitiable, Tamara drooped
onto her bed; she sobbed, then started,
suddenly, tear on rolling tear,
her bosom laboured, breath oppressed her—
when, from above, a voice addressed her;
she seemed in magic tones to hear:
"Don't weep, my child! no use in steeping
a voiceless corpse with tears unsleeping!
Such tears are no life-giving dew:
they simply cloud your eyes; such weeping
burns up complexion's virgin hue!

he's far from here, he's past all knowing,
from him your grief can earn no praise;
celestial radiance now is glowing
before his incorporeal gaze;
for him heaven's choirs are now intoning . . .
what are life's paltry dreams, the oppressed
tears of a poor young girl, her groaning,
to the celestial country's guest?
No mortal creature should be reckoned,
whatever be his lot, as worth—
believe me—for a single second,
your grief, my angel of the earth!

"On the heavens' ethereal ocean,
rudderless, without a sail,
starry choirs in ordered motion
calmly float through vapour's veil;
over heaven's unbounded spaces,
unattainable, unheard,
leaving after them no traces,
pass the clouds in fleecy herd.
Times for meeting, or leave-taking,
bring them neither joy nor pain;
future brings them no wish-making,
past, no will to live again.
In the grievous hour of sorrows,
they are what you should recall;
take no heed for earthly morrows,
be uncaring, like them all!

"As soon as night on the Caucasian
summits has cast its mantle round,
as soon as its bewitching suasion
has stilled the world, as if spellbound;

as soon as on the cliff there passes
a night wind through the withered grasses,
and hidden deep in them a bird
cheerfully in the dark has stirred;
as soon as, under vineyard railing
thirstily drinking the unfailing
dewfall, the flower of night has bloomed;
as soon as the gold moon has loomed
silently from the mountain-sill,
looked at you sidelong in the still—
then I shall fly to you and keep
tryst with you till the daystar flashes,
and on the silk of your eyelashes
I shall infuse the gold of sleep . . ."

XVI

Then the voice faded like illusion,
the sound had come, the sound died out.
She started up, she looked about . . .
and inexpressible confusion
reigned in her breast; fear, grief, joy, doubt,
compared to this were just delusion.
Her feelings bubbled up in rout;
her soul arose and snapped its shackles,
while fire came racing through each vein;
that voice, so strange it raised the hackles,
she thought she heard it speak again.
Just before daybreak, welcome-seeming
slumber had dimmed Tamara's gaze;
and yet her mind was in a daze,
astonished with prophetic dreaming.
A stranger, mute, through mists that curled,
in beauty clad not of this world,

came to her, leaned above her pillow;
and in his glance was such a billow
of love and grief that you'd infer
all his compassion was for her.
This was no angel to befriend her,
this was no heaven-sent defender:
no crown of iridescent beams
adorned his forehead with its gleams;
nor one of those who burn together
in hell, no tortured sinner—no!
he was like evening in clear weather:
not day, nor night—not gloom, nor glow!

PART II

I

"Oh, father, father, cease from chiding,
leave your Tamara free from threat;
I weep: see how my tears are gliding,
they've flowed for days, they're flowing yet.
It's futile that from distant places
suitors crowd hither to my side . . .
Georgia abounds in maiden graces;
my fate is to be no one's bride! . . .
Oh, father, throw stern words away.
You've noted how, from day to day,
victim of poison's curse, I'm fading:
an evil dream, past all evading,
torments me; there's no way to flee;
I'm lost, it's pressing down on me!
To holy sanctuary send me,
send me to cool my raging head;
for there my Saviour will defend me,

with Him my anguish will be shed.
No worldly joys can now deceive me ...
so in a shrine's protecting gloom
rather let some dim cell receive me,
an early foretaste of the tomb ..."

II

And so to a secluded holy
cloister her parents took her; dressed
in a habiliment of lowly
hairshirting was that maiden breast.
But even in her monastic twilling,
as under damask's figured gleam,
still with the same illicit dream
just as before her heart was thrilling.
At the altar, in the candle's glow,
at moments of most solemn singing,
or while the voice of prayer was ringing,
would sound those tones she had to know.
And where the dim cathedral lifted
its vaulting, often would repair,
soundless and traceless as the air,
where the thin films of incense drifted,
a starlike figure, shining there;
it called, it beckoned her ... but where?

III

Between two hills, in shade abounding,
the sacred convent hid away
in planes and poplars tight-surrounding;
sometimes, when darkness came to stay

on the ravine, a lamp, appearing
in a faint glimmer through the clearing,
revealed where that young sinner lay.
In shade that almond-trees projected,
sad crosses in their rows protected
the voiceless graves; there the small birds
in choirs of song rehearsed their words.
Over the stones ran, bubbling, springing,
fountains of water, chilled as ice,
that under beetling cliffs would slice
across the valley-bed and, singing,
tumble on further through a scrub
whose bloom hoar-frosted every shrub.

IV

To northward, mountain peaks were showing.
And when Aurora, early glowing,
watches the smoky mists of blue
rise from the valley, layer on layer,
and when, face to the east, as due,
all the muezzins call to prayer,
and the clear voice of the bell-tower
wakens the people with its shaking;
in that pacific, solemn hour
at which the Georgian maiden, taking
her long and tapering pitcher, goes
for water down the steep, there grows
a mountain range, all capped in snows;
against the limpid heaven it throws
a wall of lilac past comparing;
or in the sunset hour it's wearing
a chasuble that darkly glows;
and in the middle stands, invading

cloudland, the supreme peak by far,
Kazbek, all turbaned in brocading,
of Caucasus the mighty tsar.

V

With guilty thoughts in crowding session,
Tamara's deaf to the intercession
of honest pleasures. In her eyes
the whole world's wrapped in shade and sadness;
all things are cause for pain and madness—
night's gloom, or radiance of sunrise.
No sooner has the chill infusion
of sleepy night flowed all around,
than she in frenzy and confusion
before the icon falls to ground;
she weeps; and in the silent tension
of night her sobs with apprehension
trouble the wayfarer's attention:
"There groans some spirit of the height,
chained in a cavern, sadly stirring!"
he listens hard through the still night,
then gives his weary horse a spurring.

VI

Tamara at the window-sill
stares at the distant scene, and still
stares, languid, full of trepidation;
she sits in lonely meditation,
she sighs and waits, waits the whole day . . .
a whisper comes: he's on his way!
Her dreams, his manner of appearing,
such flattery had not failed to reach

her heart; his sad gaze, the endearing,
the tender strangeness of his speech.
Herself not knowing rhyme or reason,
she's pined and languished many days;
her heart may wish to pray in season
to holy saints, to *him* it prays;
worn out by struggle unabating,
if she lies down on slumber's bed,
her pillow burns, she's suffocating,
she starts up, shivering with dread;
her breast, her shoulders flame, she races
to breathe, she chokes, mist's in her eyes,
her arms are thirsting for embraces,
and on her lips a kiss that dies . . .

VII

Now Georgia's mountains had been vested
in aery robes of twilight hue.
Down to the cloister, as suggested
by his sweet wont, the Demon flew.
And yet he shrank, long minutes through,
he started back from violating
the peace in which that shrine was waiting.
There was a moment when he dreamed
of giving up his grim designing.
Around the high wall, brooding, pining,
he roamed: without a breeze, it seemed
the leaves had stirred from his returning.
In shade he looked up; her undone
window displays a lantern burning;
she's long been waiting for someone!
And now, amid the silence reigning,

chingar's* harmonious complaining
lilted, and strains of song began;
they flowed, these sounds, they ran and ran,
they pressed, like tears, hard on each other;
so tender was that song, you'd find
that up in heaven, for mankind,
its melodies had been designed.
Perhaps to a forgotten brother
some angel, moved to meet again,
had flown in stealth and raised this strain
to alleviate the other's pain,
songs where time past found sweet narration? . . .
Love's swooning and love's agitation—
for the first time the Demon now
experienced them; in shock and shiver
he thinks of fleeing—but no quiver
stirs in his wing! from his dimmed brow
a heavy teardrop, a slow river . . .
what marvel! till today, quite near
that cell, there stands in wondrous fashion
a stone scorched by a tear of passion,
burnt through by an inhuman tear! . . .

VIII

And, as he enters, love is winning,
his soul is opened to the good;
he thinks, for life a new beginning
has come, as he had prayed it would.
The vague alarm of expectation,
the unspoken fear of the unknown,
as if at a first confrontation

* Chingar: A kind of guitar. (*Lermontov's note.*)

to that proud soul had now been shown.
Then comes a grim prefiguration!
he enters—there in front of him
heaven's envoy, the cherubim,
radiant, on his protective mission
keeps the fair sinner from all things
evil, defends her from perdition
inside the shadow of his wings;
and sudden light, from heaven down-beating,
blinded the Demon's unclean sight;
instead of a sweet-spoken greeting,
heavy rebuke was prompt to smite:

IX

"Oh, soul of evil, soul unsleeping,
in midnight gloom, what tryst is keeping?
None of your votaries are here,
no breeze of ill has dared to roister
till now in this my well-loved cloister;
so bring no wicked footsteps near.
Who summoned you?" A crafty sneer
was Demon's manner of replying;
all red with envy was his look;
and once more in his soul, undying,
hate's poison brew began to cook.
"She's mine!" cried out the grim contender,
"release her, for you come too late,
too late to serve as her defender
and stand in judgement on her fate
or mine. On her proud soul, I tell you,
I have affixed my seal above;
so from your cloister I repel you,
this is *my* kingdom, here I love!"

And on the victim, now past saving,
the Angel cast a sorrowing eye
and slow as slow, with pinions waving,
was drowned in the ethereal sky.

. . . .

X

TAMARA

Who are you, tempter-tongue? What duty
brings you to me—from heaven? from hell?
What do you want of me? . . .

DEMON

Your beauty . . .

TAMARA

Tell me, who are you? Answer. Tell . . .

DEMON

He to whose voice with rapt attention
you listened in the still midnight,
whose grief you guessed at, whose intention
spoke to your soul, whose vague dimension
you saw in dreaming; who can blight
hopes with one glance, and bring them crashing;
whom no one loves; who lives for lashing
his earthly slaves with furious beat,
the king of freedom and cognition,
heaven's foe, and nature's own perdition,
and yet, you see him at your feet!
I bring a message of devotion,
a prayer of love; for you I've kept
my first pains of earthbound emotion,

and the first tears I ever wept.
Oh, hear me out! oh, have some notion
of pity! back to heaven you
with just a single word could send me.
With your love's raiment to defend me,
thus vested, I'd stand there, a new
angel with a new gleam to attend me;
oh, only hear me out, I pray—
I love you like a slave! the day
when I set eyes on you there started
in me a secret but whole-hearted
hatred for my immortal sway.
I found I envied such deficient
happiness as exists down here;
all life not yours was insufficient,
all life away from you brought fear.
Then in my dull heart, unexpected,
a glow began to warm and wake;
deep in an old wound and undetected,
grief started stirring like a snake.
What, without you, is life eternal?
what are my boundless realms infernal?
Just empty words, a loud discord,
a vast cathedral—with no lord!

TAMARA

Deceitful spirit, you must leave me!
Be still, I'll not believe the foe . . .
Oh, my Creator . . . grief and woe!
no prayer comes out . . . my wits deceive me,
they falter, gripped by venom's ire!
Listen, you pile up doom above me
with words of poison and of fire . . .
Tell me the reason why you love me!

DEMON

The reason why, fair one, you said?
Alas, I know it not! . . . elated
with new life, from my guilty head
the thorny crown I relegated,
threw in the ashes all my days:
my heaven, my hell are in your gaze.
I love you with no earthly passion,
such love that *you* could never find:
with rapture, in the towering fashion
of an immortal heart and mind.
On my sad soul, from world's first aeon,
deeply your image was impressed;
ever before me it progressed
through wastes of timeless empyrean.
My thoughts had long been stirred and racked
by just one name of passing sweetness:
my days in paradise had lacked
just your perfection for completeness.
If you could guess, if you could know
how much it costs in tribulation
throughout the ages' long gradation
to take one's pleasure, suffer woe,
to expect no praise for evil, no
prize for good deeds; what condemnation
to live for self, by self be bored
in endless struggle—no reward,
no crown, no reconciliation!
To regret all, to seek no prize,
to know, feel, see all things for ever,
to seek to hate the world—whatever
there may be in it, to despise! . . .
As soon as I from heaven's employment
was banned by curses, from that day

all nature's warmth and sweet enjoyment
grew chilled for ever, froze away;
bluer before me stretched the spaces;
I saw apparelled in their places,
like wedding guests, the lights I knew . . .
crowned, gliding one behind another;
and yet their former friend and brother
not one would recognise anew.
So, in despair, the expatriated,
the outcasts I began to call,
but faces, words, and looks that hated,
I failed to recognise them all.
And so, in horror, wings inflected,
I swooped away—but whither? why?
I know not . . . I had been rejected
by my old friends; like Adam I
found the world gone deaf-mute and dry.
So, at the current's free impulsion,
a helpless and storm-crippled boat,
sailless and rudderless, will float,
knowing no goal for its propulsion;
so at the earliest morning-tide
a scrap of thunder-cloud will ride,
in heaven's azure vaults the only
visible speck, unhalting, lonely,
will without trace and without sense
fly God knows whither, God knows whence!
Briefly I guided mankind's thought,
briefly the ways of sin I taught,
discredited what's noble, brought
everything beautiful to nought;
briefly . . . the flame of all committed
belief in man I firmly drowned . . .
but was it worthwhile to confound
just hypocrites and the half-witted?

I hid where the ravines run deep;
I started, meteor-like, to sweep
on course through midnight's darkest glooming . . .
A lonely wayfarer was looming,
enticed by a near lamp—to fall
over the cliff-edge, horse and all;
vainly he called out—bloody traces
followed him down the mountain-side . . .
but hatred's tricks, its sad grimaces,
brought me a solace that soon died!
How often, locked in dusty battle
with some great hurricane, in shroud
of mist and lightning I would rattle
and swoop and storm amid the cloud,
and hope in elemental churning
to stifle all my heart's regret,
to escape from thoughts that kept returning,
the unforgotten to forget!
What is the sum of the privations,
the labours and the grief of man,
of past, of future generations,
compared with just one minute's span
of all my untold tribulations?
What is man's life? his labour? why—
he's passed, he's died, he'll pass and die . . .
his hopes on Judgement Day rely:
sure judgement, possible forgiving!
but *my* sorrow is endless, I
am damned to sorrow everliving;
for it, no grave in which to doze!
sometimes, snakelike, it creeps, or glows
like flame, it crackles, blazes, rushes,
or, like a tomb, it chokes and crushes—
a granite tomb for the repose
of ruined passions, hopes and woes.

[TAMARA

Why should I share your griefs, your inner
torments? why listen to your moan?
You've sinned . . .

DEMON

Towards you, I'm no sinner.

TAMARA

Someone will hear us! . . .

DEMON

We're alone.

TAMARA

And God?

DEMON

Won't glance at us: eternal
for heaven, but not for earth, his care.

TAMARA

And punishment, and pains infernal?

DEMON

What of them, if we both are there?]

TAMARA

Sufferer, stranger-friend, unwilling—
whoever you may be—I find
your words set secret pleasure thrilling,
ceaselessly they disturb my mind.
But if there's cunning in your story,
if there's a secret, wicked goal . . .

oh, have some mercy! where's the glory
to you, what value is my soul?
In heaven's eye could I be reckoned
dearer than those you spurned instead?
they too are beauties, though unbeckoned!
as here, no mortal for a second
has dared defile their maiden bed . . .
Swear me a fateful oath . . . in anguish
I bid you swear . . . see how I languish;
you know the stuff of women's dreams!
instinctively you soothe my terrors . . .
you understand my ways, my errors—
and you'll have pity that redeems!
Swear it . . . from evil machinations
you'll cease for ever, swear it now.
Have you no oaths, no adjurations,
have you no single sacred vow? . . .

DEMON

By the first day of our creation
I swear, and by its final night,
I swear by evil's condemnation
and by the triumph of the right,
by downfall, with its bitter smarting,
by victories I dream to score,
by bliss of seeing you once more
and by the threat of once more parting.
I swear by all the souls of those
who serve me in predestined fashion,
I swear by my unsleeping foes;
by heaven, by hell, by earth's profession
of holiness, and by your head,
I swear by your last look's expression,
I swear by the first tear you shed,

the air your sweet lips are inhaling,
those silky curls that wave above,
I swear by bliss and by travailing,
I swear, believe it, by my love.
Old plans of vengeance and destruction
I have renounced, and dreams of pride;
henceforth, by evil's sly seduction
no human spirit shall be tried;
with heaven I seek to end my warring,
to live for praying and adoring,
to live for faith in all that's good.
Tears of repentance, as they should,
will from my forehead, thus deserving
your virtues, wash off heaven's brand,
and may the world, calm, unobserving,
flourish untroubled by my hand!
Till now, you've found appreciation
at your true worth from me alone:
I chose you for my adoration,
laid at your feet my realms, my throne.
I need your love, my benefaction
to you will be eternal life;
in love, just as in evil action,
I'm strong and quite unmoved by strife.
With me, free son of the ethereal,
to stellar regions you'll be whirled;
you're fated to be my imperial
consort, and first queen of the world.
Then without pity, without caring,
you'll learn to look down at the earth,
where no true bliss and no long-wearing
beauty exist, which brings to birth
only misdeeds and retribution,
where only paltry passions live;

where love and hate, without dilution
by fear, are past man's power to give.
Surely you know how short and fleeting
is human love's ephemeral rule?
just for a flash, young blood is heating—
then days go flying, blood runs cool!
Who can stand up to pain of parting,
or to new beauty's tempting gleams,
to weariness or boredom starting,
or to the waywardness of dreams?
Be sure that you were never fated,
my consort, to destroy your bloom
and fade away incarcerated,
enslaved in envy's narrow room,
amongst the cold and the small-minded,
the false friends and the open foes,
the fears, the toils that vainly grinded,
the fruitless hopes, the crushing woes.
No, pitifully, without passion,
you'll not expire, in prayer, behind
high walls, removed in equal fashion
from God, and from all human kind.
Oh, no, you wonder of creation,
a different destiny is yours;
you face a different tribulation
and different bliss in bounteous stores;
give up all previous ambition,
renounce the fate of this sad world:
instead, a lofty, splendid mission
before your eyes will be unfurled.
A host of souls who owe me duty
I'll bring, I'll throw them at your feet;
magically for you, my beauty,
handmaids will labour, deft and fleet;

for you from the eastern star I'll ravish
a golden crown; I'll take for you
from flowers the midnight dew, and lavish
upon your crown that selfsame dew;
I'll bring a sunset ray; ecstatic,
I'll clasp it, belt-like, round your waist,
with breath of healing aromatic
the airs around you will be laced;
all day the strains of heavenly playing
will lull your hearing with their tune;
I'll build you halls with an inlaying
of turquoise, rooms with amber strewn;
I'll sound the bottom of the ocean,
high up above the clouds I'll climb,
all, all, that's earthly, my devotion
will give you—love me! . . .

XI

And this time
with ardent lips so lightly grazing
he kissed her trembling mouth, and then
answered her pleas, in language dazing
with sweet temptation; once again
those mighty eyes were fixed and gazing
deep into hers. He set her blazing.
He gleamed above her like a spark
or like a knife that finds its mark.
That devil triumphed! In the dark,
alas, to her bosom the infernal
poison of his embrace could pierce.
A cry resounded, tortured, fierce,
troubling the stillnesses nocturnal.
In it were love, and pain's hard kernel,

reproaches, a last desperate prayer,
and then a hopeless, an eternal
farewell to life—all these were there.

XII

Meanwhile, alone, the watchman pacing
past the steep wall serenely made
his nightly duty-round, embracing
the iron gong that told his trade;
and near the cell of that young sinner
he slowed the measure of his tread;
above the gong his hand in inner
puzzlement poised, he halted dead.
And through the stillness all around him
he thought he heard an undertone,
two mouths that kissed, then came to astound him
a short, sharp cry, a feeble moan.
And a detestable suspicion
pierced to the old man's heart . . . but stay,
a moment passed in this condition
and all was silent; far away
only a breeze began to play
and brought the sound of leaves that rustled;
in its dark bed the torrent bustled
and sadly murmured on its way.
In fear the old night-watchman hurries
to say a text from holy writ,
and chase the wicked thought that worries
with its bad spell his sinful wit;
he crosses with his quavering fingers
a breast disturbed by reverie's force,
in silence he no longer lingers
but goes his customary course.
. . . .

XIII

Like a sweet peri sleeping lightly
she lay inside her coffin now;
cleaner than counterpane, and whitely
blooming, the dull hue of her brow.
Lowered for ever were her lashes . . .
But heavens! who would not have supposed
the eyes beneath them simply dozed
and marvellously just reposed
waiting a kiss, or daystar's flashes?
But fruitlessly the light of day
poured on them all its golden ray;
her parents' lips kissed them but vainly
in speechless sorrow. All too plainly
from them there's nothing has the power
to tear death's seal off at this hour!

XIV

Never in festal days' confusion
had sweet Tamara been so dressed,
in such bright hues, so rich a vest.
Flowers from her valley in profusion
(such is tradition's strict behest)
above her shed their perfume; pressed
in her dead hand, they looked like making
farewell to earth, a last leave-taking!
and nothing in her face implied
to onlookers how she had died
in blaze of rapture and of passion;
no, all her features were instilled
with a calm beauty that was chilled,
expressionless in marble-fashion,

blank of all thought, of feeling's breath,
impenetrable, just like death.
And a strange smile that had come fleeting
across her lips was frozen cold.
Of grief and much heartbreak, on meeting
any perceptive eye, it told:
it carried cool contempt's impression,
the scorn of one prepared to die,
it carried a last thought's expression
and, to the earth, a dumb goodbye—
of life now gone, a vain reflection,
deader than those death sets apart,
of eyes grown dim, a recollection
even more hopeless for the heart.
Just as, at sunset's grave occasion,
far on the skyline the Caucasian
snow-ranges—when in molten gold
day's chariot founders—iridescent,
their radiance for a moment hold,
in dark of distance incandescent—
and yet this half-dead light can show
no glimmer down to the benighted
desert, and no one's path is lighted
by gleams those icy summits throw.

XV

Now every neighbour, each relation,
for the sad pilgrimage is bound.
His grey locks all in laceration,
beating his breast without a sound,
for the last time Gudál has mounted
his faithful, his white-crested horse,
and the cortege begins its course.

Three days and three nights must be counted
to reach the calm refuge she shares
with bones of her long-dead forebears.
Of every traveller and each village
the scourge, an ancestor of hers,
chained down by illness, all his pillage
repented—history so avers—
wished for past crimes to win redemption,
and vowed to build a minster, right
on top of a granitic height
where blizzard's dirge had the preemption,
where no bird ventured but the kite.
And soon from Kazbek's snows a lonely
temple arose, and on the crest
the bones of that wrong-doer only
in such a scene could find new rest;
so to a graveyard was converted
that rock, the kin of clouds on high:
as if, the nearer to the sky,
the tomb was warmer ... or, averted
and shut away from human gaze,
as if death's sleep were sounder-seeming ...
vain hope! for dead men, there's no dreaming
the joys, the griefs of earlier days.

XVI

A holy Angel through ethereal
immensities of heaven's blue
winged it on golden pinions, who
was carrying off from things material
a sinful spirit as he flew.
And with sweet words of consolation
and hope he scattered all her doubt;
all trace of crime and tribulation,

with flowing tears he washed it out.
Already, from far off, there swept them
homeward the sounds of heavenly bliss—
when there flew up to intercept them
a hellish soul from the abyss.
He was as mighty as the roaring
whirlwind, as lightning did he shine;
proudly, and with insanely soaring
audacity he cried: "She's mine!"

Tamara's sinful soul was riding
tight-gripped against her guardian's breast;
by prayer her terrors were suppressed.
And now her fate was for deciding,
again he stood before her eyes,
but, God!—too changed to recognise!
so evil was the whole impression,
so full of poison and aggression
and endless hatred; in a wave
the Demon's motionless expression
breathed out the coldness of the grave.
"Begone, dark spirit of denial!"
so heaven's ambassador replied:
"for long enough your wicked pride
has triumphed—God will now decide,
for this is judgement hour; her trial
is past, the days of test by fire;
with earth's corruptible attire
from evil's thrall she's liberated.
Her soul is ours, and long-awaited!
Her spirit, one of those by right
whose life on earth is to be reckoned
a flash of sharpest pain, a second
of unattainable delight:
woven by God from an ethereal

substance are all their vital strings;
they were not made for things material,
nor made for them, material things!
In cruel, costly expiation
she has atoned for all her doubt.
She suffered love and tribulation—
and heaven for love has opened out."

The Angel, with stern gaze unsleeping,
stared at the tempter, then on high,
his pinions joyfully upsweeping,
merged in the radiance of the sky.
Vanquished, the Demon execrated
his reveries and their mad scope,
was left once more to his inflated
arrogance, left there isolated
in all the world—no love, no hope!

Above Koishaur's ravine, where climbs
the mountain through its rocky stages,
there stands, preserved to modern times,
a jagged wreck from bygone ages.
About it, tales for children's ears
too frightful, linger in tradition . . .
And voiceless as an apparition,
witness of those uncanny years,
it lifts, through trees, its blackened towers.
Below, the *aül* houses spill,
the earth is green and bright with flowers;
a hum of voices grows, falls still
lost in the distance, and the tinkling
caravan bells sound far away,
while through the vapours, gleaming, twinkling,
the river shoots in foam and spray.

And vital, youthfully eternal,
loving the sunshine and the vernal
coolness, old Nature frolics there
just like a child without a care.
But the sad castle, after giving
long years of duty-service, ends
as some poor old man does, outliving
all of his dear ones and his friends.
Only its unseen dwellers, waiting
for moonrise, then begin to stir;
then is their time for celebrating!
they buzz, they scurry, and they whirr.
A spider, anchorite-beginner,
works at his web, the grey old spinner;
up on the roof a jolly pack
of lizard families are brawling;
a canny snake from his dark crack
comes out punctiliously crawling
across the flags of the old stair;
now in three coils he gathers there,
and now in one long streak he's creeping,
just like a blade, all bright and steeled,
forgot on some old battlefield,
no use to heroes dead and sleeping! . . .
All's wild, nowhere is any trace
of years gone by: no, in this place
Time's hand has long been busy sweeping,
nothing there is that now recalls
the glorious state Gudál was keeping,
with his sweet daughter, in these halls!

But the church on the mountain-tower
where to the earth their bones were vowed,
kept safely by some sacred power,

can still be seen amidst the cloud.
By the church-door, on sentry-go,
a line of black granitic boulders,
with snowy mantles on their shoulders,
wear as breastplate against the foe
eternal ice's glittering show.
Relics of landslide, dreaming masses
like waterfalls, grooved with crevasses,
hang down where they were snapped and caught
by frost, as if in frowning thought.
And there the blizzard goes patrolling,
puffing snow-dust from those grey walls,
now setting a lament a-rolling,
now answering with sentry-calls.
And hearing in some far direction
of a famed minster in this land,
from eastward, clouds in serried band
hurry to make their genuflection;
but on that circle of tombstones
no one now weeps, and no one moans.
There Kazbek's cliff, in dour ill-humour,
locks up its booty far from harm,
and mankind's everlasting rumour
troubles not that eternal calm.

CHARLES JOHNSTON is the highly acclaimed translator of Pushkin's *Eugene Onegin* and has also published two volumes of his own poems. With his wife, formerly Princess Natasha Bagration, he translated *A Sportsman's Notebook* by Turgenev. From 1965 to 1971 he was British High Commissioner in Australia.